Dinah Zike's

Big Book of
Math

Middle School and High School

Dinah Zike, M.Ed.

Copyright ©2003, Dinah-Might Adventures, LP
Dinah-Might Adventures, LP
P.O. Box 690328
San Antonio, Texas 78269-0328
Office (210) 698-0123
Fax (210) 698-0095
Orders only: 1-800-99DINAH (993-4624)
Orders or catalog requests: orders@dinah.com
E-mail: dma@dinah.com
Website: www.dinah.com
ISBN 1-882796-19-5

Table of Contents

Dear Teacher,

In this book, you will find instructions for making Foldables as well as ideas on how to use them. They are an excellent communication tool for students and teachers.

National Math Standards and Communication Skills

The Principles and Standards for School Mathematics, published by the National Council of Teachers of Mathematics (NCTM) in 2000, stress the importance of communication skills in a strong mathematics program. Not all students will become mathematicians, engineers, or statisticians, but all students need to be able to think, analyze, and problem solve using skills acquired through the study of mathematics.

Throughout their lives, students will be called upon to be literate in mathematics— personally and professionally. They will need to have a basic understanding of numbers, operations, and quantitative reasoning; patterns, relationships, and algebraic thinking; geometry; measurement; and probability and statistics to solve real-life problems involving finances, chance, design, science, fine arts, and more.

Furthermore, students must be able to share the results of their use of mathematics using various forms of oral and written communication. Foldables are one of many techniques that can be used to integrate reading, writing, thinking, organizing data, researching, and other communication skills into an interdisciplinary mathematics curriculum.

Who, What, When, Why

You probably have seen at least one of the Foldables featured in this book used in supplemental programs or staff-deveopment workshops. Today, my Foldables are used internationally. I present workshops and keynotes to over fifty thousand teachers and parents a year, sharing the Foldables that I began inventing, design- ing, and adapting over thirty years ago. Around the world, students of all ages are using them for daily work, note-taking activities, student-directed projects, forms of alternative assessment, math journals, graphs, charts, tables, and more.

Add and Amend

After workshop presentations, participants would ask me for lists of activities to be used with the Foldables they had just learned to make. They needed help visualizing how to convert math data into Foldables. So, over fifteen years ago, I began collect- ing and sharing the ideas listed in this book. The ideas are organized by topic. The table for each topic shows the math content being addressed and an appropriate Foldable. I hope you enjoy making Foldables a part of your math classroom!

Why Use Foldables in Mathematics?

When teachers ask me why they should take time to use the Foldables featured in this book, I explain that they

. . . quickly organize, display, and arrange information, making it easier for students to grasp math concepts and master skills.

. . . result in student-made study guides that are compiled as students listen for main ideas, read for main ideas, and work their way through new concepts and procedures.

. . . provide a multitude of creative formats in which students can present projects, research, and computations instead of typical poster board or math fair formats.

. . . replace teacher-generated writing or photocopied sheets with student-generated print.

. . . incorporate the use of such skills as comparing and contrasting, recognizing cause and effect, and finding similarities and differences into daily work and long-term projects. For example, these Foldables can be used to compare and contrast student explanations and procedures for solving problems to the explanations presented by other students and teachers.

. . . continue to "immerse" students in previously learned vocabulary and concepts, providing them with a strong foundation that they can build upon with new observations, experiences, and knowledge.

. . . can be used by students or teachers to easily communicate data through graphs, tables, charts, models, and diagrams, including Venn diagrams.

. . . allow students to make their own math journals for recording main ideas, problem-solving strategies, examples, questions that arise during classwork, and personal experiences that occur during learning.

. . . can be used as alternative assessment tools by teachers to evaluate student progress or by students to evaluate their own progress.

. . . integrate language arts, the sciences, and social sciences into the study of mathematics.

. . . provide a sense of student ownership in the mathematics curriculum.

Foldable Basics

What to Write and Where

Teach students to write general information--titles, vocabulary words, concepts, questions, main ideas, and laws or theorems--on the front tabs of their Foldables. General information is viewed every time a student looks at a Foldable. Foldables help students focus on and remember key points without being distracted by other print.

Ask students to write specific information—supporting ideas, student thoughts, answers to questions, research information, computation steps, class notes, observations, and definitions—under the tabs.

As you teach, demonstrate different ways in which Foldables can be used. Soon you will find that students make their own Foldables and use them independently for study guides and projects.

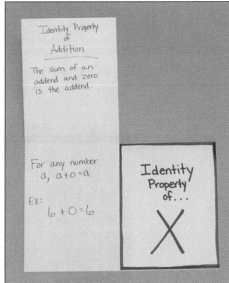

With or Without Tabs

Foldables with flaps or tabs create study guides that students can use to self check what they know about the general information on the front of tabs. Use Foldables without tabs for assessment purposes (where it's too late to self check) or projects where information is presented for others to view quickly.

Venn Diagram used as a study guide

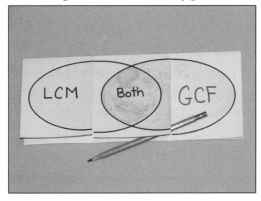

Venn Diagram used for assessment

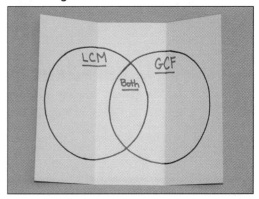

What to Do with Scissors and Glue

I don't expect secondary students to bring glue and scissors to math class. Instead, I set up a small table in the classroom and provide several containers of glue, numerous pairs of scissors (sometimes tied to the table), containers of markers and colored pencils, a stapler, clear tape, and anything else I think students might need to make their Foldables. Don't be surprised if students donate unusual markers, decorative-edged scissors, gel pens, stencils, and other art items to your publishing table.

The more they make and use graphic organizers, the faster students become at producing them.

Storing Graphic Organizers in Student Portfolios

Turn one-gallon freezer bags into student portfolios which can be collected and stored in the classroom. Students can also carry their portfolios in their notebooks if they place strips of two-inch clear tape along one side and punch three holes through the taped edge.

Have each student write his or her name along the top of the plastic portfolio with a permanent marker and cover the writing with two-inch clear tape to keep it from wearing off.

Cut the bottom corners off the bag so it won't hold air and will stack and store easily.

HINT: *I found it more convenient to keep student portfolios in my classroom so student work was always available when needed and not "left at home" or "in the car." Giant laundry-soap boxes make good storage containers for portfolios.*

Let Students Use This Book As an Idea Reference

Make this book of lists available to students to use as an idea reference for projects, discussions, extra credit work, cooperative learning group presentations, and more.

Selecting the Appropriate Foldable

Dividing Math Concepts into Parts

Foldables divide information and make it visual. In order to select the appropriate Foldable, decide how many parts you want to divide the information into and then determine which Foldable best illustrates or fits those parts. Foldables that are three-dimensional also make the student interact with the data kinesthetically.

For example, if you are studying the Fundamental Laws of Algebra you could choose a Foldable that has five tabs (or sections), on the front tabs write the laws, and under the tabs, explain the laws in words on one side, and in symbols on the other side.

Math Concepts Already Divided into Parts

Algebra		*Geometry*		*Statistics and Probability*	
Parts	**Concept**	**Parts**	**Concept**	**Parts**	**Concept**
5	Fundamental Laws	2	collinear and noncollinear	3	mean, median,mode
3	parentheses, brackets, and braces	2	complementary and supplementary angles	1	Fundamental Counting Principal
2	equalities and inequalities	2	convex and concave	4	Who, What, When, Where: Blaise Pascal
2	numeric and algebraic expressions	3	translation, rotation, reflection	2	linear permutations and circular permutations
2	domain and range	6	types of triangles	2	upper quartile and lower quartile
7	properties of addition and multiplication	4	SSS, SAS, ASA, AAS	2	permutations and combinations
2	LCM and LCD	2	two types of right triangles	2	dependent and independent events
3	monomials, binomials, and trinomials	6	types of quadrilaterals	2	odds in favor and odds against
2	powers and exponents	2	x-axis and y-axis	2	mutually inclusive and exclusive events

Math Concepts That Can Be Divided into Parts

Algebra	*Geometry*	*Statistics and Probability*
write algebraic expressions	draw angles with a protractor	determine ranges of sets
evaluate expressions	classify polygons	interpret scatter plots
sequence steps	illustrate quadrilaterals	display data collected in plots
list algebraic rules	list examples of prisms	draw models of combinations
solve equations	name ordered pairs	
find values for variables	graph points	

Dividing Skills and Foldables into Parts

Reading, writing, and thinking skills can easily be used with Foldables. The following lists show examples of skills and activities and a selection of Foldables divided into parts. You may want to refer to this page as you select activities from the lists of math topics in the third section of this book (see pages 35–92).

Skills and Activities Divided into Parts

1 Part	2 Parts
Find the Main Idea	Compare and Contrast
Predict an Outcome	Cause and Effect
Narrative Writing	Similarities and Differences
Descriptive Writing	Opposite Operations
Expository Writing	
Persuasive Writing	

3 Parts	4 Parts
Venn Diagrams	Who, What, When, Where
Know?-Like to Know?-Learned?	What, Where, When, Why/How
Beginning, Middle, End	

Any Number of Parts	
Questioning	Making and Using Tables
Flow Charts	Making and Using Graphs
Vocabulary Words	Making and Using Charts
Time Lines	Sequencing Data or Events
Concept Webs or Maps	

Foldables Divided into Parts

1 Part	2 Parts
Half Book	Two-Tab Book
Folded Book	Pocket Book
Three-Quarter Book	Shutterfold
Large Matchbook	Matchbook Cut in Half
Bound Book	Concept Map with Two Tabs

3 Parts	4 Parts
Trifold Book	Four-Tab Book
Three-Tab Book	Standing Cube
Pyramid Book	Top-Tab Book
Layered-Look Book	Four-Door Book
Concept Map with Three Tabs	

Any Number of Parts	
Accordion Book	Circle Graph
Layered-Look Book	Concept-Map Book
Sentence-Strip Holder	Vocabulary Book
Folded Table, Chart, or Graph	Time-Line Book
Pyramid Mobile	Bound Book
Top-Tab Book (three or more sheets of paper)	Multiple-Pocket Books

Basic Foldable Shapes

The following figures illustrate the basic folds that are referred to throughout the following section of this book .

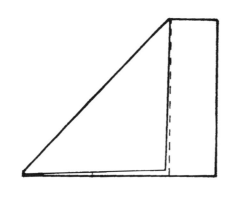

Taco Fold

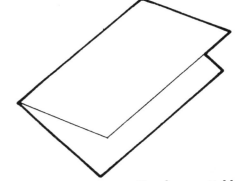

Hamburger Fold

Hot Dog Fold

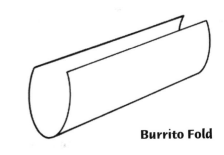

Burrito Fold

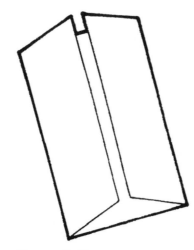

Shutter Fold

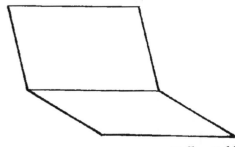

Valley Fold

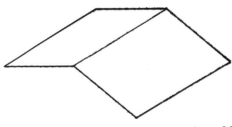

Mountain Fold

Half-Book

Fold a sheet of paper (8 1/2" × 11") in half.

1. This book can be folded vertically like a *hot dog* or . . .

2. . . . it can be folded horizontally like a *hamburger.*

Use this book for descriptive, expository, persuasive, or narrative math writing, as well as graphs, diagrams, or charts.

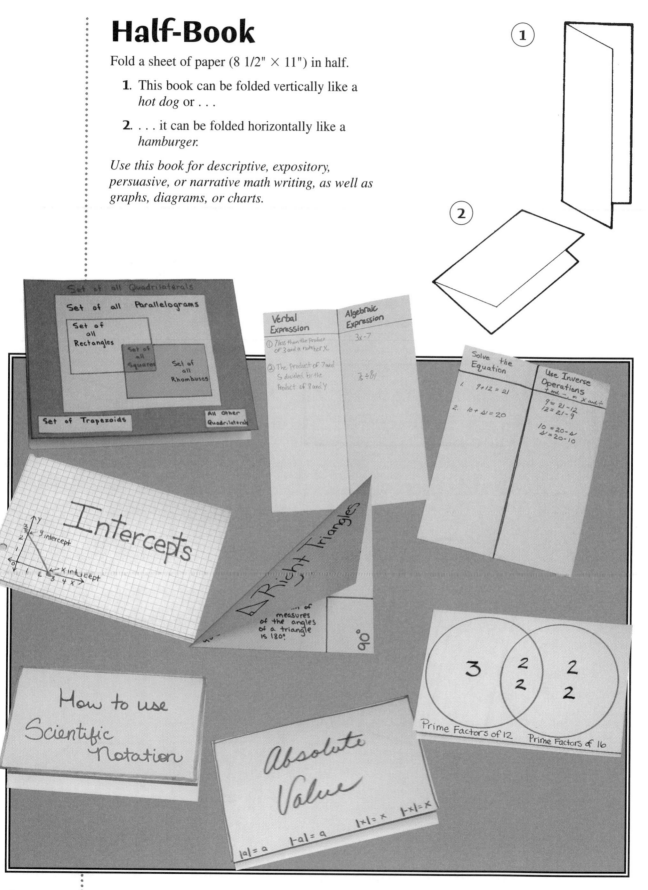

Folded Book

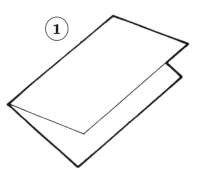

1. Make a *half-book*.

2. Fold it in half again like a *hamburger*. This makes a ready-made cover, and two small pages for information on the inside.

Use photocopied work sheets, Internet print outs, and student-drawn diagrams or maps to make this book. One sheet of paper becomes two activities and two grades.

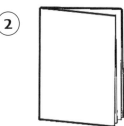

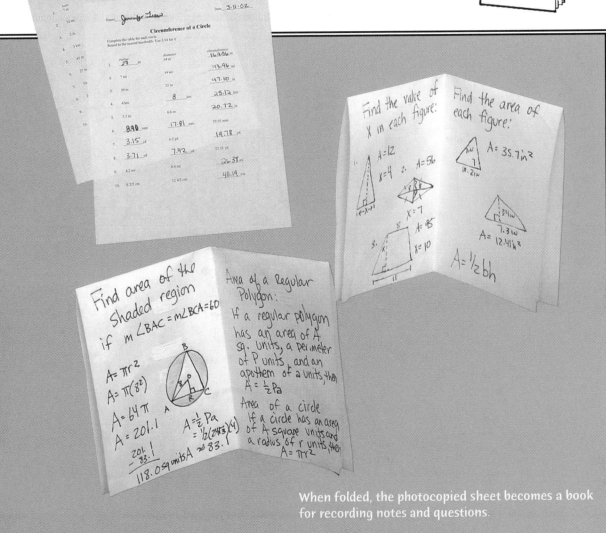

When folded, the photocopied sheet becomes a book for recording notes and questions.

Bound Book

1. Take two sheets of paper (8 1/2" × 11") and separately fold them like a *hamburger*. Place the papers on top of each other, leaving one sixteenth of an inch between the *mountain tops*.

2. Mark both folds one inch from the outer edges. When using notebook paper to make this journal, the margins are marked one inch from the outer edges.

3. On one of the folded sheets, cut from the top and bottom edge to the marked spot on both sides.

4. On the second folded sheet, start at one of the marked spots and cut the fold between the two marks.

5. Take the cut sheet from step 3 and fold it like a *burrito*. Place the *burrito* through the other sheet and then open the *burrito*. Fold the bound pages in half to form an eight-page book.

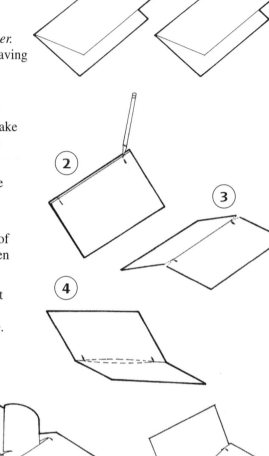

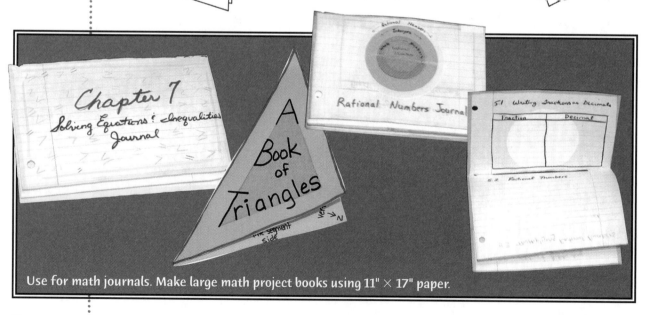

Use for math journals. Make large math project books using 11" × 17" paper.

Two-Tab Book

1. Take a *folded book* (see pg.12) and cut up the *valley* of the inside fold toward the *mountain top*. This cut forms two large tabs that can be used front and back for writing and illustrations.

2. The book can be expanded by making several of these folds and gluing them side-by-side.

Use this book for data that occurs in twos, for example opposite operations.

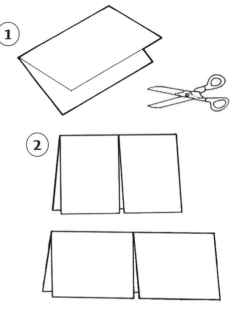

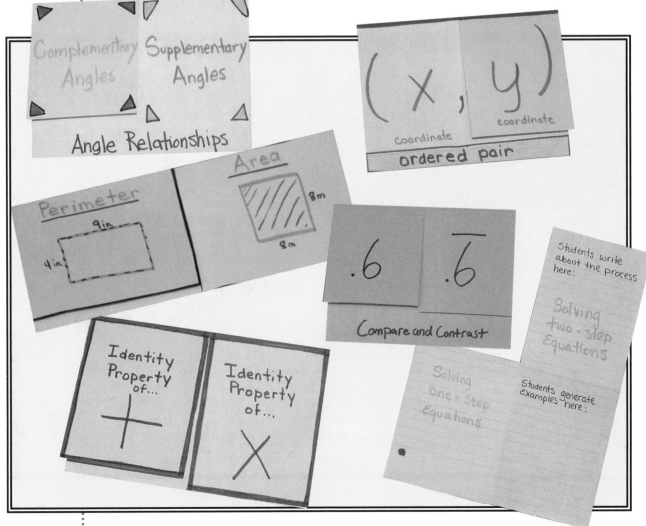

Matchbook

1. Fold a sheet of paper (8 1/2" × 11") like a *hamburger,* but fold it so that one side is one inch longer than the other side.

2. Fold the one-inch tab over the short side forming an envelopelike fold.

3. Cut the front flap in half toward the *mountain top* to create two flaps.

Use this book to report on one or two vocabulary words, questions, or concepts. Collect matchbooks and use them to make great student-made bulletin boards.

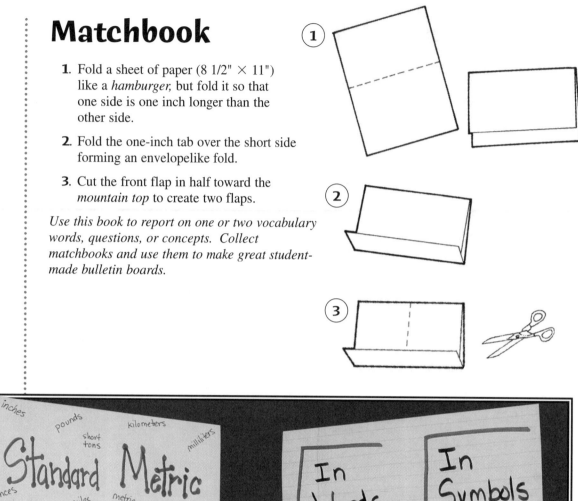

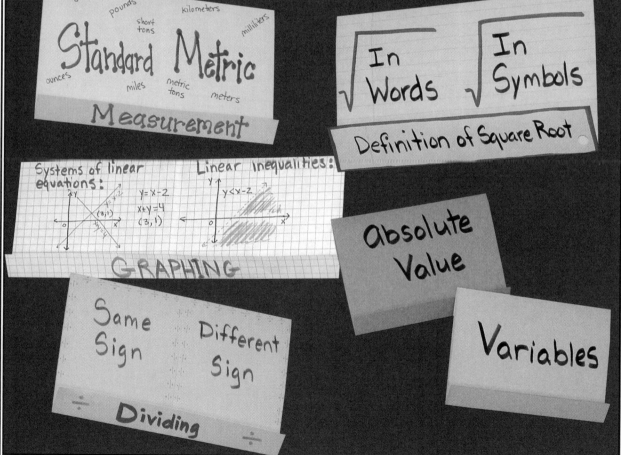

Pocket Book

1. Fold a sheet of paper (8 1/2" × 11") in half like a *hamburger.*

2. Open the folded paper and fold one of the long sides up two inches to form a pocket. Refold along the *hamburger* fold so that the newly formed pockets are on the inside.

3. Glue the outer edges of the two-inch fold with a small amount of glue.

4. **Optional:** Glue a cover around the *pocket book.*

   Variation: Make a multi-paged booklet by gluing several pockets side-by-side. Glue a cover around the multi-paged *pocket book.*

Use 3" × 5" index cards or quarter sheets of notebook paper inside the pockets. Store student-made books, such as two-tab books and folded books in the pockets.

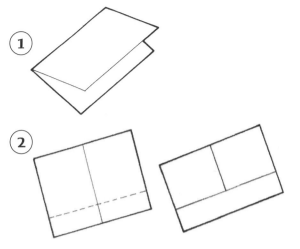

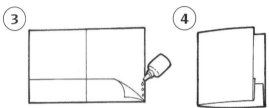

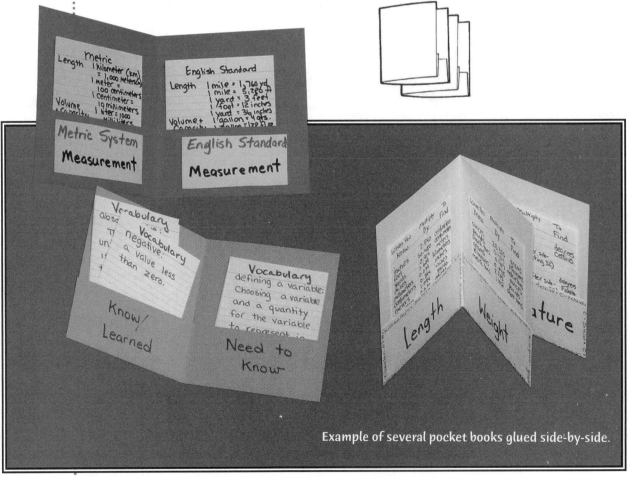

Example of several pocket books glued side-by-side.

Shutter Fold

1. Begin as if you were going to make a *hamburger* but instead of creasing the paper, pinch it to show the midpoint.

2. Fold the outer edges of the paper to meet at the pinch, or mid-point, forming a *shutter fold.*

Use this book for data occurring in twos. Or, make this fold using 11" × 17" paper and smaller books—such as the half book, journal, and two-tab book—that can be glued inside to create a large project full of student work.

Trifold Book

1. Fold a sheet of paper (8 1/2" × 11") into thirds.

2. Use this book as is, or cut into shapes. If the trifold is cut, leave plenty of fold on both sides of the designed shape, so the book will open and close in three sections.

Use this book to make charts with three columns or rows, large Venn diagrams, or reports on data occurring in threes.

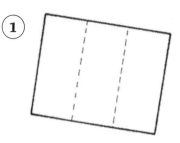

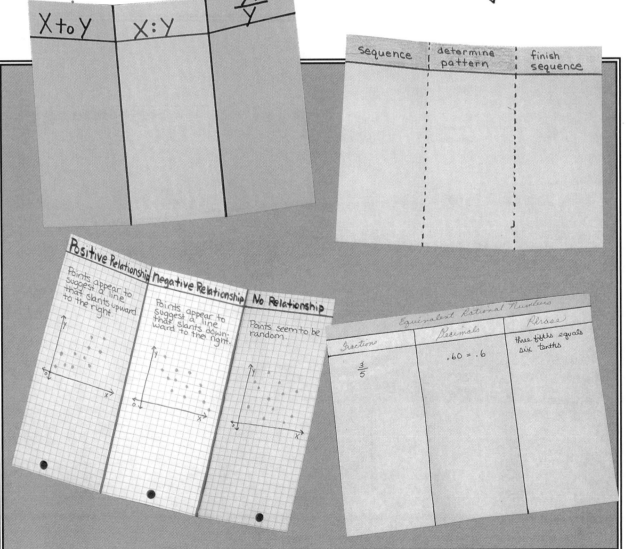

Three-Tab Book

1. Fold a sheet of paper like a *hot dog.*

2. With the paper horizontal, and the fold of the *hot dog* up, fold the right side toward the center, trying to cover one half of the paper.

   NOTE: *If you fold the right edge over first, the final graphic organizer will open and close like a book.*

3. Fold the left side over the right side to make a book with three folds.

4. Open the folded book. Place your hands between the two thicknesses of paper and cut up the two *valleys* on one side only. This will form three tabs.

Use this book for data occurring in threes, and for two-part Venn diagrams.

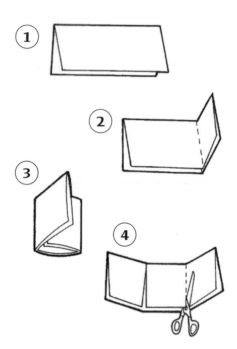

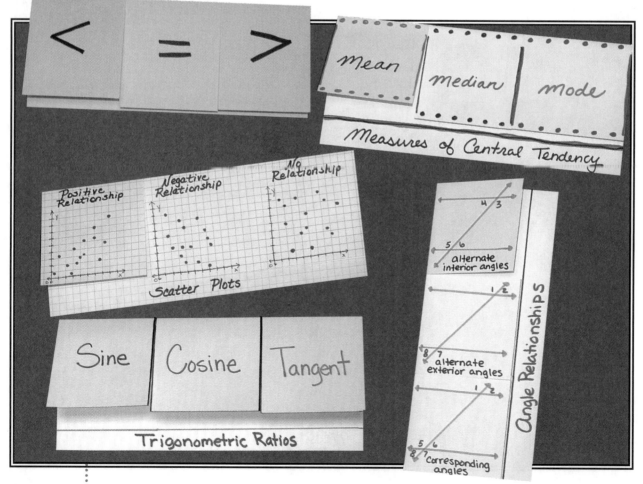

Three-Tab Book Variations

VARIATION A:
Draw overlapping circles on the three tabs to make a Venn Diagram

VARIATION B:
Cut each of the three tabs in half to make a six-tab book.

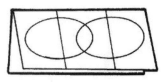

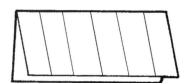

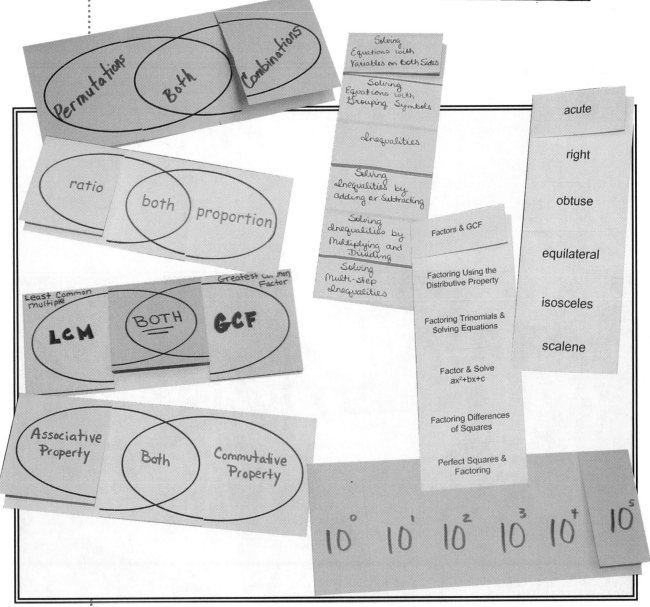

Pyramid Fold

1. Fold a sheet of paper (8 1/2" × 11") into a *taco,* forming a square. Cut off the excess rectangular tab formed by the fold.

2. Open the folded *taco* and refold it the opposite way forming another *taco* and an X-fold pattern.

3. Cut one of the folds to the center of the X, or the midpoint, and stop. This forms two triangular-shaped flaps.

4. Glue one of the flaps under the other, forming a *pyramid.*

5. Label front sections and write information, notes, thoughts, and questions inside the pyramid on the back of the appropriate tab.

Use to make mobiles and dioramas. Use with data occurring in threes.

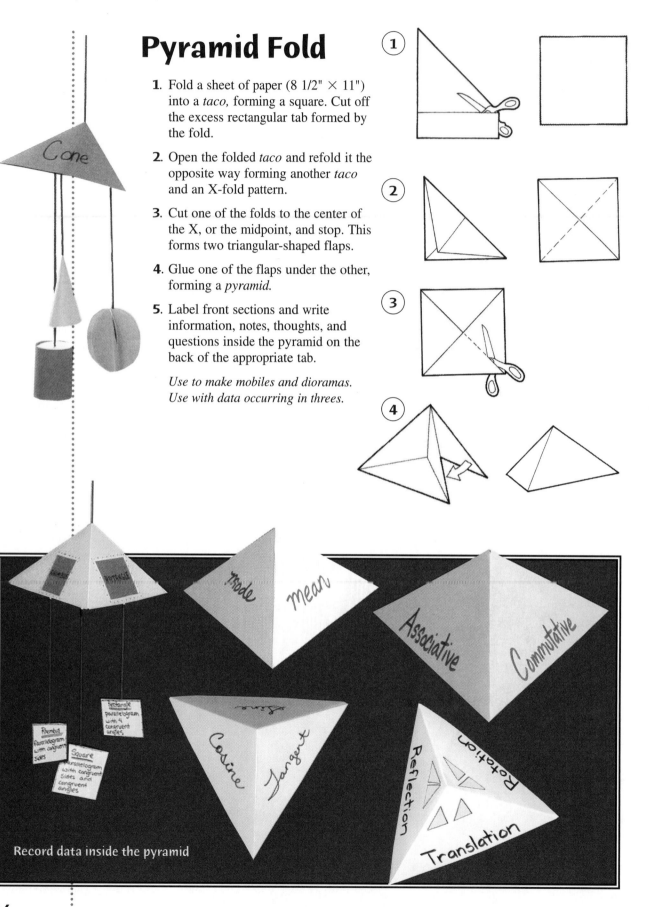

Record data inside the pyramid

Layered-Look Book

1. Stack two sheets of paper (8 1/2" × 11") so that the back sheet is one inch higher than the front sheet.

2. Bring the bottom of both sheets upward and align the edges so that all of the layers or tabs are the same distance apart.

3. When all tabs are an equal distance apart, fold the papers and crease well.

4. Open the papers and glue them together along the *valley* or inner center fold or, staple them along the mountain.

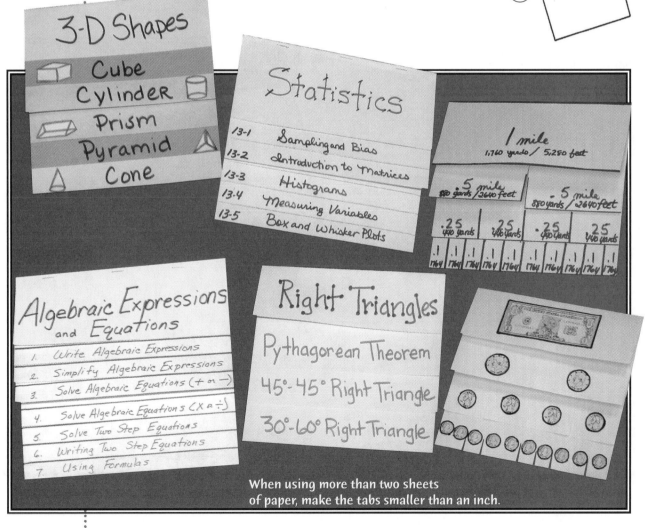

When using more than two sheets of paper, make the tabs smaller than an inch.

Four-Tab Book

1. Fold a sheet of paper (8 1/2" × 11") in half like a *hot dog*.

2. Fold this long rectangle in half like a *hamburger*.

3. Fold both ends back to touch the *mountain top* or fold it like an *accordion*.

4. On the side with two *valleys* and one *mountain top*, make vertical cuts through one thickness of paper, forming four tabs.

Use this book for data occurring in fours. For example: the four steps in the order of operations.

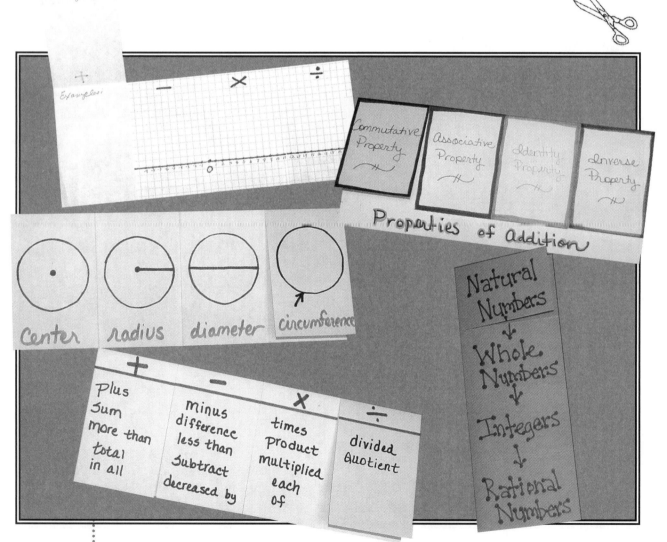

Envelope Fold

1. Fold a sheet of paper (8 1/2" × 11") into a taco forming a square. Cut off the excess paper strip formed by the square.

2. Open the folded taco and refold it the opposite way forming another taco and an X fold pattern.

3. Open the taco fold and fold the corners toward the center point of the X forming a small square.

4. Trace this square on another sheet of paper. Cut and glue it to the inside of the envelope. Pictures can be placed under or on top of the tabs, or can be used to teach fractional parts.

Use this book for data occurring in fours. For example, four operations.

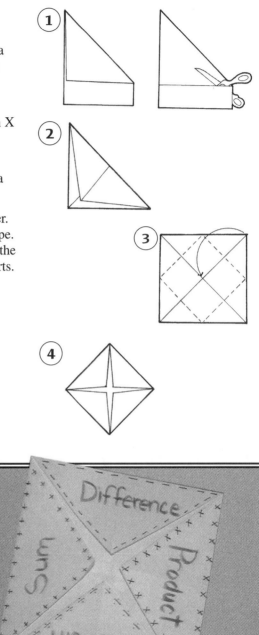

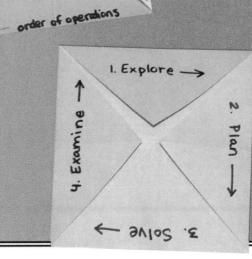

Standing Cube

1. Use two sheets of the same size paper. Fold each like a *hamburger*. However, fold one side one half inch shorter than the other side. This will make a tab that extends out one half inch on one side.

2. Fold the long side over the short side of both sheets of paper, making tabs.

3. On one of the folded papers, place a small amount of glue along the the small folded tab, next to the *valley* but not in it.

4. Place the non-folded edge of the second sheet of paper square into the *valley* and fold the glue-covered tab over this sheet of paper. Press flat until the glue holds. Repeat with the other side.

5. Allow the glue to dry completely before continuing. After the glue has dried, the cube can be collapsed flat to allow students to work at their desks. The cube can also be folded into fourths for easier storage, or for moving it to a display area.

Use with data occurring in fours or make it into a project. Make a small display cube using 8 1/2" × 11" paper. Use 11" × 17" paper to make large project cubes that you can glue other books onto for display. Notebook paper, photocopied sheets, magazine pictures, and current events also can be displayed on the large cube.

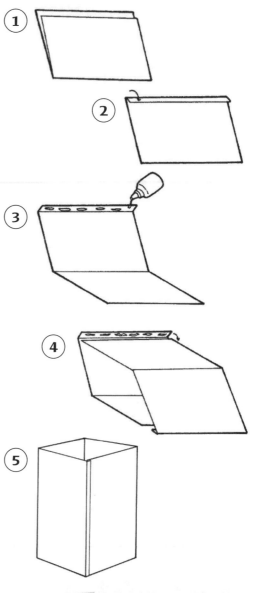

This large cube project can be stored in plastic bag portfolios.

Four-Door Book

1. Make a *shutter fold* (see pg.12) using 11" × 17" or 12" × 18" paper.

2. Fold the *shutter fold* in half like a *hamburger.* Crease well.

3. Open the project and cut along the two inside *valley* folds.

4. These cuts will form four doors on the inside of the project.

Use this fold for data occurring in fours. When folded in half like a hamburger, a finished four-door book can be glued inside a large (11" × 17") shutter fold as part of a larger project.

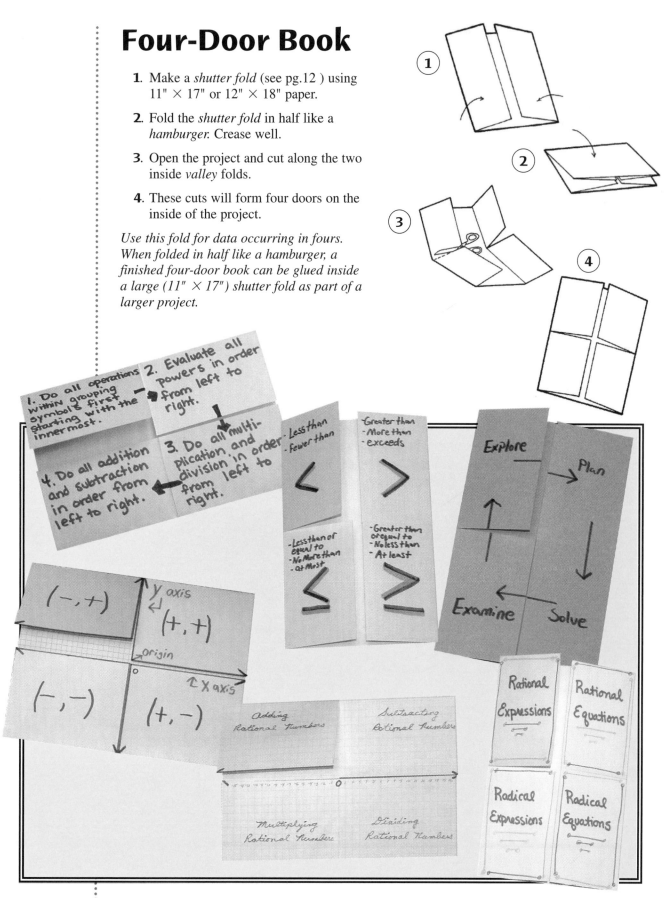

Top-Tab Book

1. Fold a sheet of paper (8 1/2" × 11") in half like a *hamburger.* Cut the center fold, forming two half sheets.

2. Fold one of the half sheets four times. Begin by folding in half like a *hamburger,* fold again like a *hamburger,* and finally again like a *hamburger.* This folding has formed your pattern of four rows and four columns, or 16 small squares.

3. Fold two sheets of paper (8 1/2" × 11") in half like a *hamburger.* Cut the center folds, forming four half sheets.

4. Hold the pattern vertically and place on a half sheet of paper under the pattern. Cut the bottom right hand square out of both sheets. Set this first page aside.

5. Take a second half sheet of paper and place it under the pattern. Cut the first and second right hand squares out of both sheets. Place the second page on top of the first page.

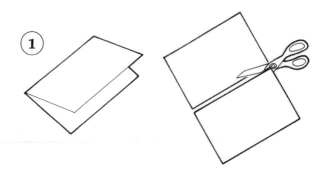

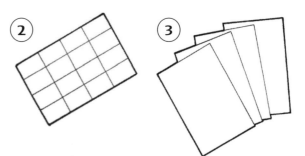

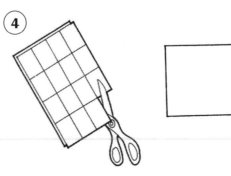

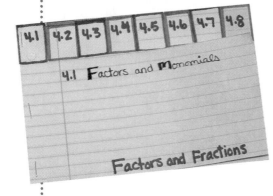

6. Take a third half sheet of paper and place it under the pattern. Cut the first, second, and third right hand squares out of both sheets. Place this third page on top of the second page.

7. Place the fourth, uncut half sheet of paper behind the three cut out sheets, leaving four aligned tabs across the top of the book. Staple several times on the left side. You can also place glue along the left paper edges, and stack them together. The glued spine is very strong.

8. Cut a final half sheet of paper with no tabs and staple along the left side to form a cover.

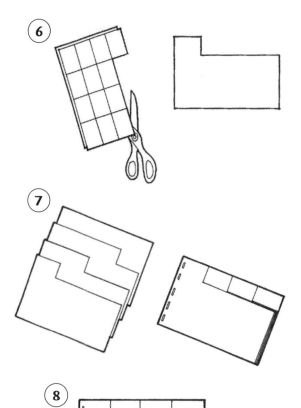

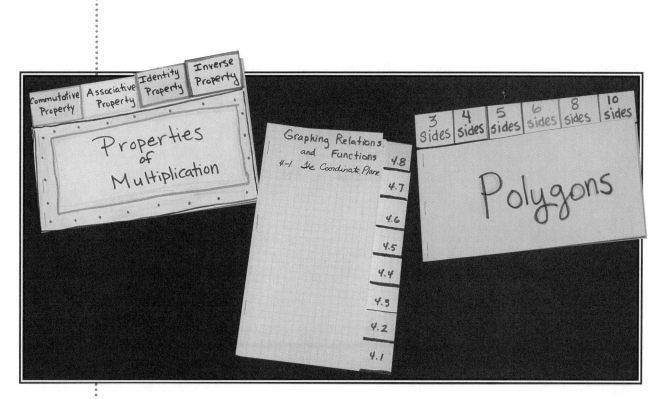

Accordion Book

NOTE: *Steps 1 and 2 should be done only if paper is too large to begin with.*

1. Fold the selected paper into *hamburgers*.

2. Cut the paper in half along the fold lines.

3. Fold each section of paper into *hamburgers*. However, fold one side one half inch shorter than the other side. This will form a tab that is one half inch long.

4. Fold this tab forward over the shorter side, and then fold it back away from the shorter piece of paper (in other words, fold it the opposite way).

5. Glue together to form an *accordion* by gluing a straight edge of one section into the *valley* of another section.

NOTE: *Stand the sections on end to form an accordion to help students visualize how to glue them together. (See illustration.)*

Always place the extra tab at the back of the book so you can add more pages later.

Use this book for number lines, timelines, student projects that grow, sequencing events or data, and more.

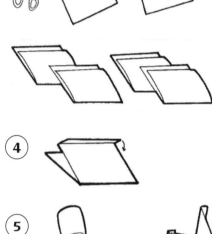

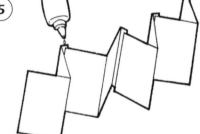

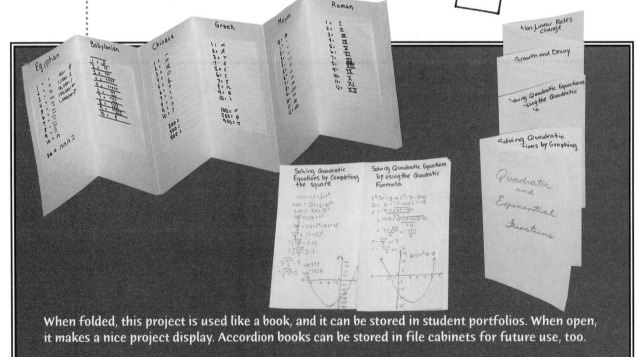

When folded, this project is used like a book, and it can be stored in student portfolios. When open, it makes a nice project display. Accordion books can be stored in file cabinets for future use, too.

Pop-Up Book

1. Fold a sheet of paper (8 1/2" × 11") in half like a *hamburger*.

2. Beginning at the fold, or *mountain top*, cut one or more tabs.

3. Fold the tabs back and forth several times until there is a good fold line formed.

4. Partially open the *hamburger* fold and push the tabs through to the inside.

5. With one small dot of glue, glue figures for the *pop-up book* to the front of each tab. Allow the glue to dry before going on to the next step.

6. Make a cover for the book by folding another sheet of paper in half like a *hamburger*. Place glue around the outside edges of the *pop-up book* and firmly press inside the *hamburger* cover.

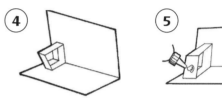

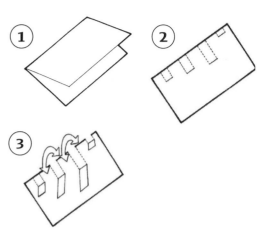

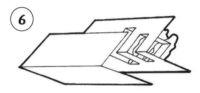

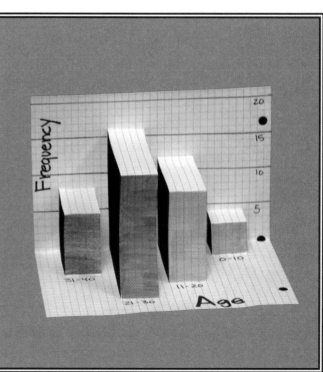

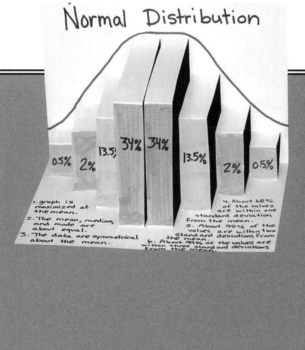

Folding into Fifths

1. Fold a sheet of paper in half like a hotdog or hamburger for a five tab book, or leave open for a folded table or chart.

2. Fold the paper so that one third is exposed and two thirds are covered.

3. Fold the two thirds section in half.

4. Fold the one third section backward to form fifths. The paper will be divided into fifths when opened.

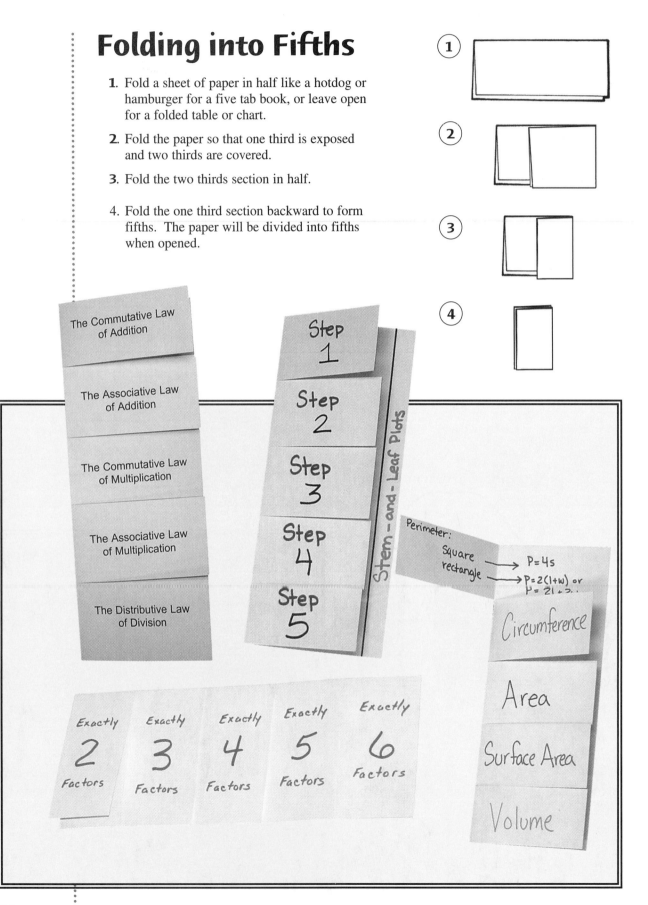

Folded Table, Chart, or Graph

1. Fold the number of vertical columns needed to make the table or chart.

2. Fold the horizontal rows needed to make the table or chart.

3. Label the rows and columns.

REMEMBER: *Tables are organized along vertical and horizontal axes, while charts are organized along one axis, either horizontal or vertical.*

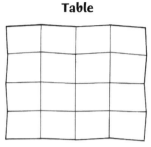

Table

Chart

Monomials	+	−	×	÷
Polynomials				

	Ratio	Proportion	Percent	Decimal	Fraction
Define	a comparison of two numbers by division	a statement of equality of two ratios	a percent is a ratio that compares a number to 100		
Example A					
Example B					
Example C					

Learning About 3-D Figures	Prisms	Cylinders	Pyramids	Cones
Volume	rectangular prism $V = lwh$ 125 ft³	$V = \pi r^2 h$	$V = \frac{1}{3} Bh$	$V = \frac{1}{3} \pi r^2 h$
Surface Area				

distance	rate	time	d = rt

Metric Prefix	Common Unit	Exponent	Symbol
kilo	1,000	10^3	K
hecto	100	10^2	h
deka	10	10^1	da
	1	10^0	m, g, L, m²
deci	.1	10^{-1}	d
centi	.01	10^{-2}	c
milli	.001	10^{-3}	m

Sequence	Next ④ Terms
1.25 1.45 1.65 +0.20 +0.20	1.85 2.05 2.25 2.45 +0.20 +0.20 +0.20
1 3 7 +2 +4 +6	13 21 31 43 +8 +10 +12

27

Folding a Circle into Tenths

1. Fold a paper circle in half.

2. Fold the half circle so that one third is exposed and two thirds are covered.

3. Fold the one third (single thickness) backward to form a fold line.

4. Fold the two thirds section in half.

5. The half circle will be divided into fifths. When opened, the circle will be divided into tenths.

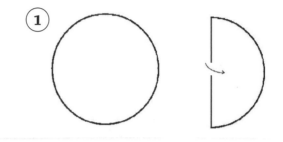

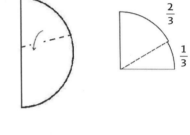

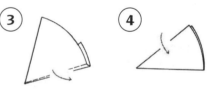

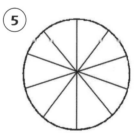

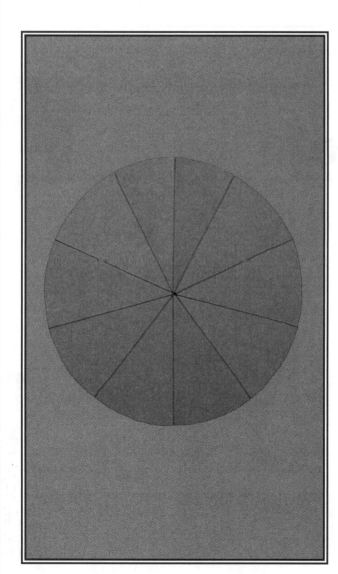

NOTE: *Paper squares and rectangles are folded into tenths the same way. Fold them so that one third is exposed and two thirds is covered. Continue with steps 3 and 4.*

Circle Graph

1. Cut out two circles using a pattern.

2. Fold one of the circles in half on each axis, forming fourths. Cut along one of the fold lines (the radius) to the middle of each circle. Flatten the circle.

3. Slip the two circles together along the cuts until they overlap completely.

4. Spin one of the circles while holding the other stationary. Estimate how much of each of the two (or you can add more) circles should be exposed to illustrate given percentages or fractional parts of data. Add circles to represent more than two percentages.

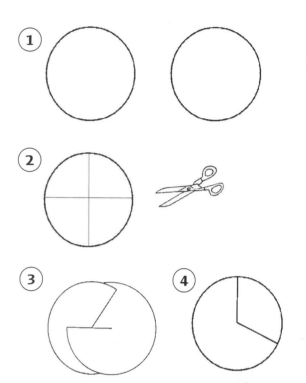

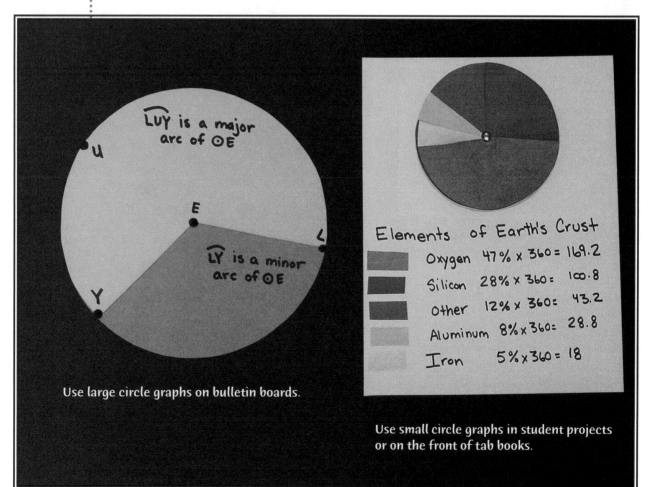

Use large circle graphs on bulletin boards.

Use small circle graphs in student projects or on the front of tab books.

Concept-Map Book

1. Fold a sheet of paper along the long or short axis, leaving a two-inch tab uncovered along the top.

2. Fold in half or in thirds.

3. Unfold and cut along the two or three inside fold lines.

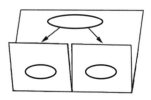
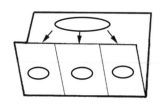

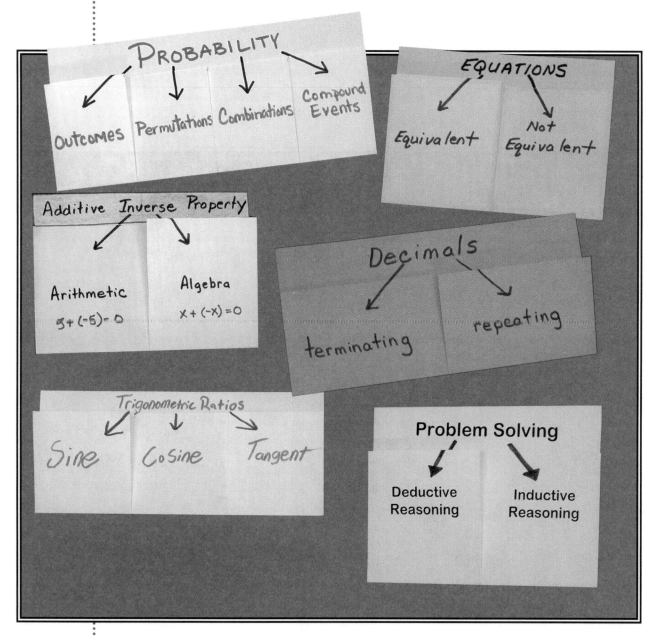

Vocabulary Book

1. Fold a sheet of notebook paper in half like a *hotdog*.

2. On one side, cut every third line. This usually results in ten tabs.

3. Label the tabs.

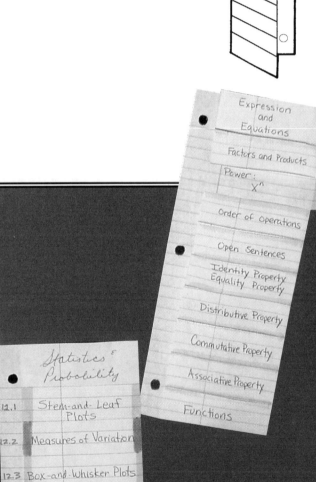

Points
Lines
Planes
Rays
Segments
Angles
Parallel
Perpendicular
Skew Lines
Degree

Expression and Equations
Factors and Products
Power: X^n
X = base
n = exponent
Order of Operations
Open Sentences
Identity Property
Equality Property
Distributive Property
Commutative Property
Associative Property
Functions

Statistics & Probability
12.1 Stem-and-Leaf Plots
12.2 Measures of Variation
12.3 Box-and-Whisker Plots
12.4 Histograms
12.5 Misleading Statistics
12.6 Counting Outcomes
12.7 Permutations and Combinations
12.8 Odds
12.9 Probability of Compound Events

Use to take notes and record data.

Leave the notebook holes uncovered and the Foldable can be stored in a notebook.

Use for vocabulary books.

Use for recording student questions and answers.

Billboard Project

1. Fold all pieces of the same size of paper in half like *hamburgers*.

2. Place a line of glue at the top and bottom of one side of each folded billboard section and glue them edge-to-edge on a background paper or project board. If glued correctly, all doors will open from right to left.

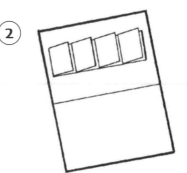

3. Pictures, dates, words, etc., go on the front of each billboard section. When opened, writing or drawings can be seen on the inside left of each section. The base, or the part glued to the background, is perfect for more in-depth information or definitions.

Use for timelines or sequencing data and number lines.

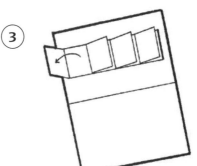

Sentence-Strip Holder

1. Fold a sheet of paper (8 1/2" × 11") in half like a *hamburger*.

2. Open the *hamburger* and fold the two outer edges toward the *valley*. This forms a *shutter fold*.

3. Fold one of the inside edges of the shutter back to the outside fold. This fold forms a floppy "L."

4. Glue the floppy L-tab down to the base so that it forms a strong, straight L-tab.

5. Glue the other shutter side to the front of this L-tab. This forms a tent that is the backboard for the flashcards or student work to be displayed.

6. Fold the edge of the L-tab up one quarter to one half to form a lip that will keep the student work from slipping off the holder.

Glue down

Use these holders to display student work on a table, or glue them onto a bulletin board to make it interactive.

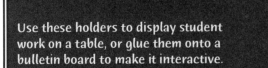

Sentence Strips

1. Take two sheets of paper (8 1/2 × 11) and fold into hamburgers. Cut along the fold lines.making four half sheets. (Use as many half sheets as necessary for additional pages to your book.)

2. Fold each sheet in half like a hotdog.

3. Place the folds side-by-side and staple them together on the left side.

4. One inch from the stapled edge, cut the front page of each folded section up to the mountain top. These cuts form flaps that can be raised or lowered.

To make a half-cover, use a sheet of construction paper one inch longer than the book. Glue the back of the last sheet to the contruction paper strip leaving one inch, on the left side, to fold over and cover the original staples. Staple this half-cover in place.

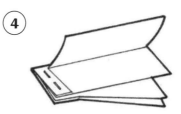

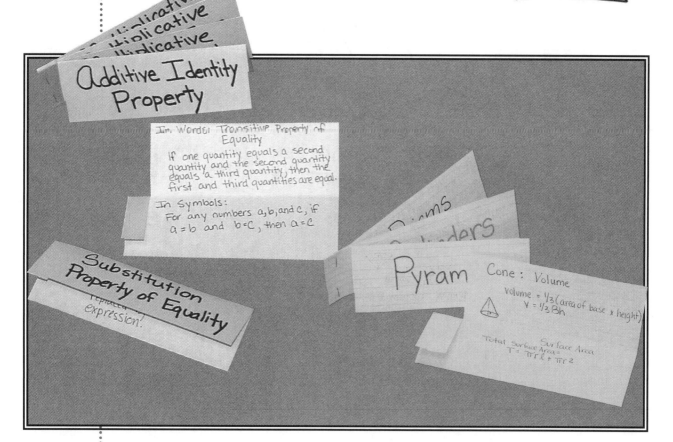

Math Activities Using Foldables

Math Activities using Foldables

Whole Numbers

Skill	Activity Suggestion	Foldable Parts
define	whole numbers as the counting numbers (0, 1, 2, 3. …) and list examples	2
explain	why fractions such as $\frac{3}{3}$, $\frac{4}{4}$, and $\frac{8}{8}$ are whole numbers	1
find	10 examples of equivalent whole numbers: $3, \frac{9}{3}$	10
describe	the two basic operations that can be performed on whole numbers: addition (combines individual numbers) and multiplication (combines groups of numbers) subtraction and division as the inverse operations of addition and multiplication	2
explain and use	the Commutative Property of Addition and the Commutative Property of Multiplication. the Associative Property of Addition and the Associative Property of Multiplication	4
outline	the Distributive Property, also called the Distributive Property of Multiplication over Addition	1
differentiate between	the Commutative Property, Associative Property, and the Distributive Property	3
define	sum, difference, product, and quotient as they relate to whole numbers	4
determine	if subtraction and division are associative (neither are) and explain your answer	2
list and describe	the order in which operations should be performed: multiply and/or divide then add and/or subtract	2
compare and contrast	two types of whole numbers: primes and composites	2
note and explain	every whole number is either prime or composite except for 0 and 1 which are neither	1
give	examples of prime factors for six whole numbers	6
reduce	given fractions to see what whole number they represent: $\frac{12}{4}, \frac{18}{9}$	any number
determine	whole numbers are greater than, less than, or equal to other whole numbers	3
round	whether five whole numbers to the nearest ten, nearest hundred, nearest thousand	5
demonstrate	three ways whole numbers can be written	3
use	whole numbers to solve real-world problems	any number
Venn diagram	characteristics of prime numbers, composite numbers, and both	3

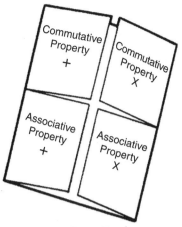

Four-Door Book

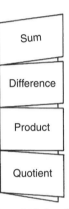

Four-Tab book

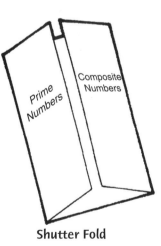

Shutter Fold

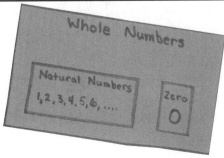

Three-Tab Venn diagram

Integers

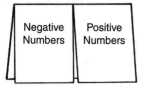

Two-Tab Book

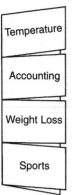

Four-Tab Book

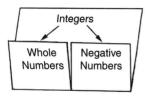

Two-Tab Concept Map

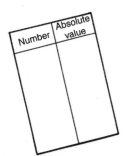

Folded Chart

Number Line

Skill	Activity Suggestion	Foldable Parts
define	integers as the set of whole numbers and their opposites, or negative numbers (...−3, −2, −1, 0, 1, 2, 3...)	1
differentiate between	positive and negative numbers	2
list	examples of positive and negative integers	2
explain	in your own words why you think zero is neither positive nor negative, but part of the set of integers	1
show	how the set of integers might be written {... −3, −2, −1, 0, 1, 2, 3, ...} and explain the use of ellipses	2
describe	four examples of the use of negative numbers in the real world: temperature, balancing account books, reporting weight loss, distance lost in a game or sport	4
define	absolute value as the number of units a number is from 0 on a number line	1
write	the definition of absolute value in words and symbols	2
find	the absolute value of given expressions	any number
explain	why absolute value can never be less than 0	1
describe	absolute value in terms of distance and give examples	2
graph	given integers on a number line	any number
	two points on a number line so that the coordinates of both have an absolute value of a given number	any number
write	inequalities using integers	any number
sequence	given integers from greatest to least, or from least to greatest	any number
state	which integers have the greater absolute value	any number
describe	how to determine if one integer is less than or greater than another integer	?
design	a concept map that shows integers as the union of whole numbers and their opposites	2
make	a number line for whole numbers and integers	1

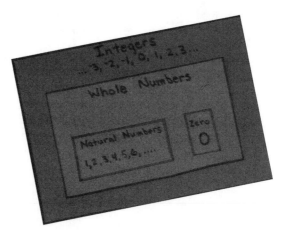

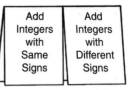

Two-Tab Book

Integers: Adding and Subtracting

Skill	Activity Suggestion	Foldable Parts
describe	how to add integers with the same sign	1
use	a number line and show how to add integers with the same sign	2
explain	how to add integers with different signs	1
use	a number line and show how to add integers with different signs	any number
compare and contrast	adding integers with the same and different signs	2
draw	a model that shows how to find the sum of two integers on a number line and describe your model	2
explain	how adding and subtracting are inverse operations that "undo" each other	2
use	a number line to show what happens when you add opposites like −9 and 9	any number
define	an integer and its opposite as additive inverses of each other	1
describe	additive inverse in words, numerically, and algebraically	3
explain	how to subtract integers using what you know about additive inverses	1
describe	how to subtract an integer in words, numerically, and algebraically	3
draw	a model that shows how to find $7 - (-2)$	1
simplify	expressions such as $15x - 18x$	any number

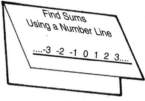

Half Book

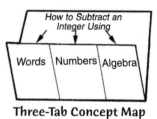

Three-Tab Concept Map

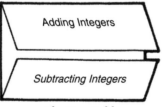

Shutter Fold

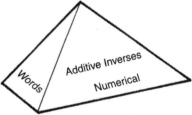

Pyramid Fold

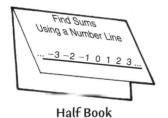

Shutter Fold

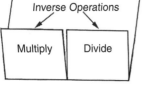

Matchbook

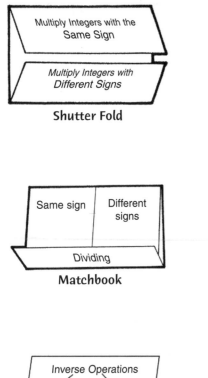

Two-Tab Concept Map

Integers: Multiplying and Dividing

Skill	Activity Suggestion	Foldable Parts
describe	how to multiply integers with the same sign	1
use	a number line to show and explain how to multiply integers with the same sign	any number
explain	how to multiply integers with different signs	1
use	a number line to show and explain how to multiply integers with different signs	2
compare and contrast	multiplying integers with the same and different signs	2
draw	a model that shows how to find the product of two integers on a number line and write about the process	2
review	how multiplying and dividing are inverse operations that "undo" each other	2
explain	how to divide integers with the same sign	1
demonstrate	how to divide integers with different signs	1
describe	how to divide integers with the same and different signs in words, numerically, and algebraically	3
find	similarities and differences between multiplying and dividing integers with the same signs and multiplying and dividing integers with different signs	4

Half Book

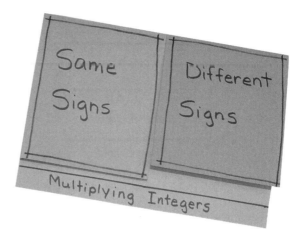

Rational Numbers

Skill	Activity Suggestion	Foldable Parts
define	rational numbers as numbers that can be written as a ratio, or fraction where *a* and *b* are integers and *b* is not equal to 0	1
explain	why whole numbers, integers, fractions, mixed numbers, terminating decimals, and repeating decimals are rational numbers	6
chart	and list examples of whole numbers, integers, fractions, terminating decimals, and repeating decimals	5
document	five rational numbers encountered in a day	5
rename	10 rational numbers	10
write	decimals as fractions and fractions as decimals	2
solve	equations using rational numbers	any number
design	a concept map for rational numbers. rational numbers: fractions, repeating and terminating decimals, integers, and whole numbers	5
estimate	sums of rational numbers	any number
find	sums of rational numbers	any number
solve	equations involving rational numbers	any number
	inequalities involving rational numbers	any number
explain	how adding and subtracting rational numbers follow the same principles as adding and subtracting integers	2
use	rational numbers to write three examples of the Commutative Property	3
	rational numbers to write three examples of the Associative Property	3
	rational numbers to write three examples of the Identity Property	3
	rational numbers to write three examples of the Inverse Property	3

Two-Tab Book

Vocabulary Book

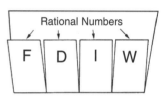

Concept Map

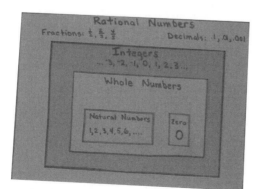

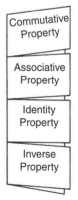

Four-Tab Book

Rational Numbers: Fractions

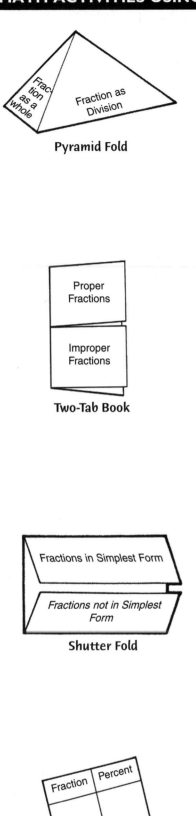

Pyramid Fold

Two-Tab Book

Shutter Fold

Folded Chart

Skill	Activity Suggestion	Foldable Parts

define	fractions three ways:
	  as part of a whole
	  as multiplication $\left(\frac{3}{5} \text{ means } 3 \text{ times } \frac{1}{5}\right)$
	  as division $\left(\frac{3}{5} \text{ means } 3 \text{ divided by } 5\right)$
		3

differentiate between	proper and improper fractions	2
rename	whole numbers as improper fractions with a given denominator	2
order	ten fractions from least to greatest	10
graph	five fractions on a number line	5
use	a number line to determine if fractions are equivalent	any number
express	six ratios as fractions in simplest form	6
determine	if five fractions are in their simplest form by checking to see if the GCF of the numerator and the denominator is 1	5
list	examples of fractions in simplest form and fractions that are not in simplest form	any number
explain	why it is easier to compare fractions with the same denominator	1
describe	how the least common denominator of fractions could be used to compare them	1
define	a mixed number as the sum of a whole number and a fraction	1
write	mixed numbers as improper fractions and improper fractions as mixed numbers	2
compare	fractions and decimals	2
chart	equivalent fractions and decimals	2
Venn diagram	given specific examples, compare characteristics of like fractions, unlike fractions, and both	3
explain	how to add like and unlike fractions in words and symbols	4
add	fractions with like and unlike denominators	2
subtract	fractions with like and unlike denominators	2
explain	how to subtract fractions with like and unlike denominators	2
compare and contrast	adding and subtracting unlike fractions	2
multiply	fractions with like and unlike denominators	2
explain	how to multiply fractions with like and unlike denominators in words and symbols	4
divide	fractions with like and unlike denominators	2
prove	that dividing by 2 is the same as multiplying by $\frac{1}{2}$, its multiplicative inverse	2
write	word problems that contain fractions	any number
express	given fractions as percents	2
tell	how you know if a fraction is greater than 100% or less than 1%	1
compare and contrast	a fraction and an algebraic fraction	2
write	six algebraic fractions in simplest form	6

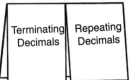

Terminating Decimals | Repeating Decimals

Two-Tab Book

Rational Numbers: Decimals

Skill	Activity Suggestion	Foldable Parts
order	ten decimals from least to greatest	10
rename	five decimals as fractions	5
explain	why decimals can be written as fractions with denominators that are powers of ten	1
find	equivalent decimals and fractions	2
differentiate	between terminating decimals, repeating decimals, and decimals that do not terminate nor repeat	3
compare and contrast	terminating and repeating decimals	2
find	examples of decimals that do not terminate or repeat	any number
write	four fractions as terminating or repeating decimals	4
define	terminating decimals	1
describe	repeating decimals	1
Venn diagram	characteristics of terminating decimals, repeating decimals, both	3
estimate	sums of six decimals using rounding and describe each	6
find	six sums of decimals and describe the process	6
estimate	six differences of decimals and write about the process	6
find	six differences of decimals and explain the process	any number
state	additive inverses of five decimals example: 8.45 and −8.45	5
illustrate	the rule for placement of the decimal point when multiplying decimals	1
explain	in your own words how to divide by a decimal	1
simplify	four expressions with decimals and explain each step	4
evaluate	five expressions with decimals and explain each step	5

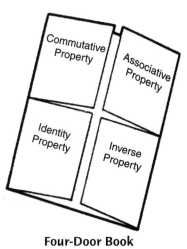

Commutative Property | Associative Property

Identity Property | Inverse Property

Four-Door Book

Terminating | Both | Repeating

Three-Tab Venn Diagram

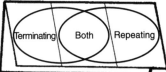

Decimals

Terminating | Repeating | Neither

Three-Tab Concept Map

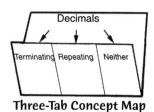

Decimals

1.0

.50

.25 .25 .50

.25 .25

.125 .125 .125 .125 .125 .125 .125 .125

Percents

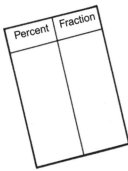

Folded Chart

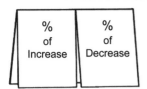

Two-Tab Book

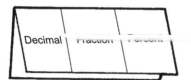

Three-Tab Book

Half Book

Bound Book

Skill	Activity Suggestion	Foldable Parts
define	percent as a ratio that compares a number to 100 or tells how many out of 100	1
explain	why percent also means hundredths, or per hundred	1
write	five percents as fractions and explain	5
use	the percent symbol when writing percents	any number
	equations to solve problems with percents	any number
make a table	that expresses decimals and fractions as percents	3
	that expresses percents as decimals and fractions	3
describe	times when it is more advantageous to use percent and times when it is more advantageous to use fractions	2
use	the percent proportion to write five fractions as percents	5
solve	six problems involving percents	6
find	the percent proportion of four numbers and explain Example: find 10% of 160	4
estimate	three percents and outline the process	3
solve	two percent problems with percent equations and sequence the steps	2
	two real-world problems involving percent	2
write	expressions for percents	any number
use	percents to estimate	any number
explain	how to estimate $x\%$ of a number	1
list	five examples of percents used in everyday life such as weather bureau's rain prediction, interest rates, discounts, and commissions and explain their use	5
describe	percent of change as the ratio of the amount of change to the original amount	1
differentiate	between percent of increase and percent of decrease	2
calculate	percent of increase and percent of decrease	2

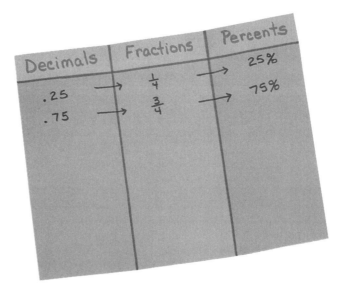

Ratios

Skill	Activity Suggestion	Foldable Parts
define	ratio as a comparison of two numbers by division	1
write	four ratios four different ways Example: 2 to 3, 2:3, $\frac{2}{3}$, and 2 ÷ 3	4
	five ratios as fractions in simplest form	5
	expressions for five ratios	5
describe	rate as a ratio that is a comparison of two measurements with different units of measurement	1
Venn diagram	characteristics of ratios, rates, and both	3
make a table	that shows five or more ratios and rates as fractions in simplest form	5+
give	three examples of unit rate	3
express	given ratios as unit rates	any number
research	the history of the golden ratio and explain its purpose	2
investigate and discover	three examples of how the golden ratio has been used over the last 4000 years to create art and architecture Example: Pyramid of Khufu in Giza	3
describe	the golden ratio in your own words	1
define	a scale drawing as a drawing that is either smaller or larger than the actual object and give examples of scale drawings	2
explain	scale as the ratio of the lengths on a drawing to the actual lengths of an object	1

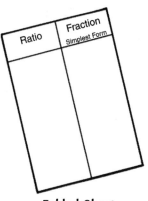

Folded Chart

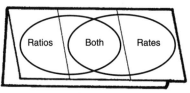

Three-tab Venn diagram

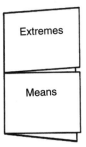

Two-Tab Book

Proportions

Skill	Activity Suggestion	Foldable Parts
define	proportion as two equal fractions, or an equivalent relationship between two ratios	1
solve	given proportions	any number
determine	if two ratios form a proportion by checking their cross products Example: ratios, check, results	3
state	the property of proportions in your own words	1
define	extremes and means	2
demonstrate	how cross products can be used to tell whether two fractions form a proportion	any number
use	proportions to solve real-world problems	any number
	proportions to estimate populations	any number
Venn diagram	ratios, proportions, both	3
explain	pi as a constant of proportionality and give examples	2

Pyramid Fold

Terms and Examples
Ratio
Rate
Unit Rate
Golden Ratio
Scale
Proportion
pi = Constant Proportion

Layered Book
(4 sheets of paper)

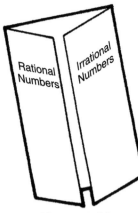

Shutter Fold

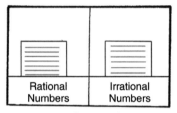

Pocket Book

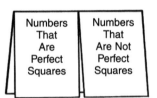

Two-Tab Book

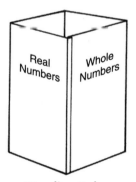

Standing Cube

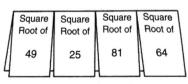

Four-Tab Book

Irrational Numbers

Skill	Activity Suggestion	Foldable Parts
define	irrational numbers as numbers that cannot be expressed as fractions $\frac{a}{b}$, where a and b are integers and b does not equal 0	1
explain	irrational numbers in words and symbols	2
determine	whether three given numbers are rational or irrational and explain your reasoning	3
compare and contrast	rational and irrational numbers	2
give examples	of irrational numbers that are less than -15	any number
describe	why pi and the square root of 3 are examples of irrational numbers	2

Real Number System

Skill	Activity Suggestion	Foldable Parts
design a concept map	that shows the set of real numbers is composed of the set of rational numbers and the set of irrational numbers	2
identify	numbers in the real number system	any number
explain	in words and symbols the real number system	2
Venn diagram	the real number system	3
chart	numbers into the categories of whole number, integer, rational, irrational, and real squares and square roots	6
define	a square root as one of two equal factors of a number	1
describe	a square root in words and symbols	2
find	the square root of 49, 25, 81, and 64	4
estimate	square roots	any number
solve	equations by finding square roots	any number
compare and contrast	numbers that are and are not perfect squares	2

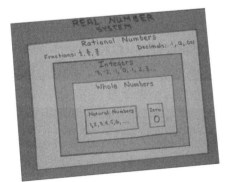

Sets and Variables

Skill	Activity Suggestion	Foldable Parts
define	a variable as a placeholder used in algebra	1
speculate	as to why variables are usually letters	1
explain	how the use of a variable can help solve algebra problems	1
define	like terms as terms with the same variable	1
compare and contrast	a numeric expression and an algebraic expression, or expressions with and without variables	2
chart	expressions in words and symbols, numerically, and algebraically	3 or 4
state	the Substitution Property of Equality (For all numbers a and b, if $a = b$, then a may be replaced with b.)	1
demonstrate	the use of the Substitution Property of Equality	1
show	multiplication and division notations used with variables	2
write	the meaning of several algebraic expressions	any number
evaluate	expressions containing variables	any number
translate	verbal phrases into algebraic expressions using variables	2
write	verbal phrases for given algebraic expressions	2
chart	words that can be used to denote addition, subtraction, multiplication, and division when reading or writing algebraic expressions	4
describe	the use of the following symbols in algebra: parentheses, brackets, and braces	3
compare	an independent variable and a dependent variable	2
research	the "who, what, when, where" of: Georg Cantor (1845–1918) developer of the theory of sets	4

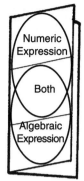

Three-Tab Venn Diagram

Three-Tab Book

Independent Variable | Dependent Variable

Two-Tab Book

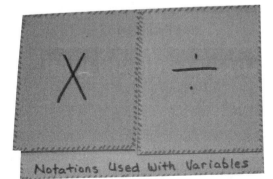

Notations Used With Variables

Algebraic Expression | Written Expression

Folded Chart

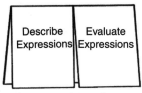

Two-Tab Book

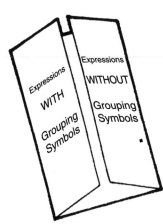

Shutter Fold

Expressions

Skill	Activity Suggestion	Foldable Parts
define	a mathematical expression as any combination of numbers and operations such as addition, subtraction, multiplication, and division	1
describe	what it means to evaluate an expression	1
demonstrate	how an expression can have several numerical values	any number
explain	why it is important to have an order of operations when evaluating expressions	1
sequence	the steps used to find the value of an expression	any number
evaluate	expressions without grouping symbols using the order of operations	2
	expressions with grouping symbols using the order of operations	2
demonstrate	how the order of operations can be changed using grouping symbols	any number
illustrate	the use of brackets [ ] and parentheses ( )	2
write	ten expressions and find their values	10
show	different ways to indicate multiplication in an expression	2
	different ways to indicate division in an expression	any number
select	three numbers and use them to write as many expressions as you can	3
compare and contrast	expressions with and without variables	2
explain	that an expression is in its simplest form when it has no like terms and no parentheses	1
chart	expressions that are and are not in their simplest form	2
describe	radical expressions and give examples	2
explain	how to add, subtract, multiply and divide radical expressions	4

Three-Tab Book

Two-Tab Matchbook

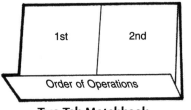

Properties

Skill	Activity Suggestion	Foldable Parts
write	the Commutative and Associative Properties of Addition and Multiplication numerically and algebraically	4
use	the Commutative Properties of Addition and Multiplication to evaluate expressions	2
rewrite	expressions using the Commutative Property	2
use	the Associative Properties of Addition and Multiplication to evaluate expressions	2
rewrite	expressions using the Associative Property	any number
compare and contrast	the Associative and Commutative Properties	2
describe	the importance of the Identity Properties of Addition and Subtraction	2
describe and use	the Zero Product Property	2
make a table	to show seven properties of addition and multiplication	7
write	the Distributive Property in words and numerically	2
read	the expression $a(b + c)$ as "a times the quantity b plus c"	1
describe	in your own words the purpose of the Distributive Property	1
rewrite	expressions different ways using the Distributive Property	any number
restate	expressions using the Distributive Property	any number
show	how the Distributive Property can be used to simplify expressions with like terms	1
make a table	to describe and give examples of: Commutative Property of Addition Commutative Property of Multiplication Associative Property of Addition Associative Property of Multiplication Identity Property of Addition Identity Property of Multiplication Zero Product Property	any number
use	the Product Property of Radicals and the Quotient Property of Radicals to evaluate expressions	2

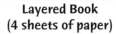

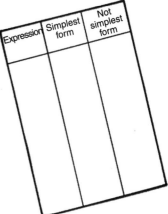

Layered Book (4 sheets of paper)

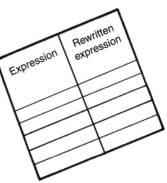

Folded Chart

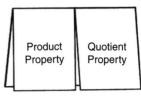

Layered Book (3 sheets of paper)

Additive Identity Property

Product Property | Quotient Property

Two-Tab Book

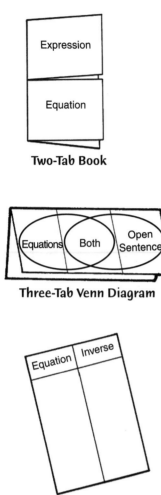

Two-Tab Book

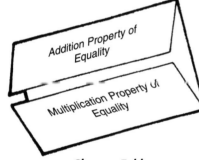

Three-Tab Venn Diagram

Folded Chart

Shutter Fold

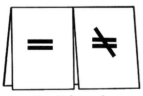

Two-Tab Book

Equations

Skill	Activity Suggestion	Foldable Parts
differentiate between	an expression and an equation	2
compare	an equation to a balance	2
Venn diagram	characteristics of equations, open sentences, and both	3
list	examples of equations	any number
tell	about equations that have no solution, or have a solution set that is null or empty	2
draw	two symbols that represent the empty or null set	2
compare and contrast	solution sets that are never true and solution sets that are always true	2
explain	why equations that contain variables are called open sentences	1
find	values for variables that make equations true	any number
explain	the solution of an equation	1
solve	equations with variables and write about how you found the solution	2
chart	solutions and open sentences	2
solve	equations with variables on each side	any number
	equations using inverse operations	any number
describe	how inverse operations "undo" each other	1
write	inverse operations for addition equations	2
	inverse operations for subtraction equations	2
solve	equations using the Addition Property of Equality	any number
solve	equations using the Subtraction Property of Equality	any number
write	examples of equations that are and are not equivalent	2
explain	when to use the Addition Property of Equality to solve an equation and give examples	?
solve	equations using the Division Property of Equality	any number
	equations using the Multiplication Property of Equality	any number
	six equations using rational numbers	6
	six equations with variables on each side	6
	six equations with grouping symbols	6
	ten equations that have an infinite number of solutions	10
explain	what is meant by the root, or roots, of three equations	3
use	integers in equations	any number
solve	equations containing rational numbers	any number
	equations with two or more operations	any number
write	five verbal problems for equations with two or more operations	5

Inequalities

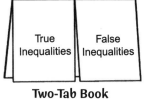

Two-Tab Book

Skill	Activity Suggestion	Foldable Parts
define	inequalities as mathematical sentences that contain greater than or less than symbols	1
write	inequalities that are true and inequalities that are false	2
	inequalities that are open, or contain a variable that must be replaced with a number	any number
chart	inequalities that are true, false, and open	3
explain	inequality signs that are a combination of the equals sign and the inequality symbols	2
chart	common phrases that are heard in everyday life that correspond to inequalities	any number
Venn diagram	methods for solving equations, inequalities, and both	3
solve	ten inequalities	10
write	sentences for inequalities and translate sentences into inequalities	2
	five inequalities and graph the solutions	5
solve	inequalities mentally	any number
state	in your own words the Addition Property of Inequality and give two examples	2
explain	the Subtraction Property of Inequality to someone	1
solve	inequalities by using the Addition and Subtraction Properties of Inequality	2
describe	the Addition and Subtraction Properties of Inequality in words and symbols	4
write	the Multiplication and Division Properties of Inequalities in words and symbols	4
solve	inequalities by multiplying or dividing by a positive number	2
	inequalities by multiplying by a negative number	2
solve	inequalities that involve more than one operation	2
Venn diagram	method for solving an inequality involving multiplication, and for solving an inequality involving division, both	3
use	inequality symbols when comparing fractions	any number
solve	inequalities containing rational numbers	any number
Venn diagram	solving an inequality with rational numbers, solving an inequality involving integers	3
solve	inequalities with multiple steps	any number
write	verbal problems with inequalities	any number
describe	a compound inequality as two inequalities connected by "or" or "and" and give examples	2

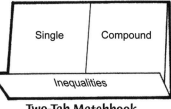

Three-Tab Venn Diagram

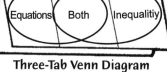

Folded Chart

Two-Tab Matchbook

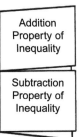

Two-Tab Book

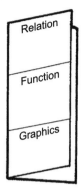
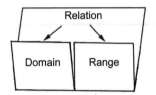

Three-Tab Book

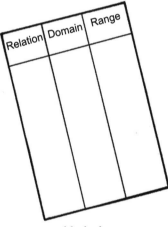

Two-Tab Concept Map Book

Folded Chart

Factors Multiples

Two-Tab Book

Relations and Functions Journal

Bound Book

Relations and Functions

Skill	Activity Suggestion	Foldable Parts
define	relations, functions, and graphing	3
Venn diagram	all functions are relations, but not all relations are functions	3
make	a concept map to show a relation as domain and range	2
write	the domain and range of given relations	3
define	function as a relation in which each element of the domain is paired with exactly one element in the range	1
graph	five relations to determine if they are functions	5
determine	whether four relations are functions by using the vertical line test	4
use	functions to describe relationships between two quantities	2
make	function tables	any number
use	function tables to find output values	any number
describe	the inverse of a relation	1

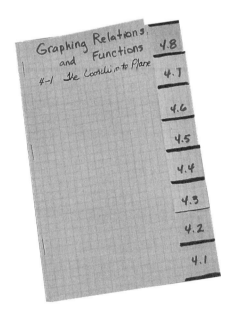

Factors

Skill	Activity Suggestion	Foldable Parts
explain	that the factors of a whole number divide that number with a remainder of 0	1
use	the phrase "divisible by" when describing the factors of a given number	1
determine	whether one number is a factor of another	any number
make a chart	of divisibility rules, examples, and descriptions	3
differentiate between	even and odd numbers and explain how they relate to factors	2
describe	multiplication facts as they relate to factors	1
explain	why 1 is a factor of every nonzero number	1
mentally determine	what five numbers are divisible by Example: 27, 64, 189, 370, 455	5
chart	numbers with exactly 2, 3, 4, 5, and 6 factors	5
define	the greatest common factor of two or more numbers as the greatest factor these numbers have in common	1
list	the factors of three sets of numbers and find the greatest factor each set has in common	3
read	GCF as the "greatest common factor"	1
use	prime factorization to find the GCF of a set of numbers	any number
explain	how the product of the common prime factors of two or more monomials is their GCF	1
Venn diagram	find the GCF of two numbers by making a Venn diagram of their factors	3
define	relatively prime numbers as numbers with 1 as their only common factor	1
determine	whether given pairs of numbers are relatively prime	any number
define	a prime number as a whole number greater than one that has exactly two factors, one and itself	1
	a composite number as a whole number greater than one that has more than two factors	1
differentiate between	prime and composite numbers	2
prove	that a composite number can always be expressed as a product of two or more products	any number
explain why	0 and 1 are considered neither prime nor composite	2
list	the factors of 1 and explain your list	1
describe	every whole number greater than 1 is either prime or composite	1

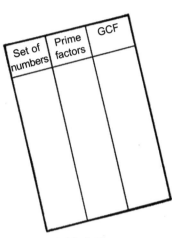

Two-Tab Book

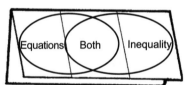

Folded Chart

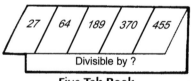

Three-Tab Venn Diagram

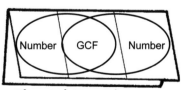

Five-Tab Book

Three-Tab Venn Diagram

Multiples of
2
3
4
5
6
7
8
9
10

Layered Book
(5 sheets of paper)

Multiples

Skill	Activity Suggestion	Foldable Parts
define	a multiple of a number as a product of that number and a whole number	1
chart	the multiples of 2, 3, 4, 5, 6, 7, 8, 9, and 10	9
differentiate	between factors and multiples	2
find	the common multiples of two numbers such as 2 and 5	2
determine	the least common multiple of two numbers	2
read	LCM as Least Common Multiple	1
use	a Venn diagram to find the LCM of two numbers using their prime factorization	3
find	the LCM of a set of numbers or algebraic expressions	any number
read	LCD as Least Common Denominator	1
find	the LCD for given pairs of fractions	any number
Venn diagram	finding a LCM, finding a LCD, both	3
explain	why fractions need the same denominator to be compared	1
find	factors and multiples	2

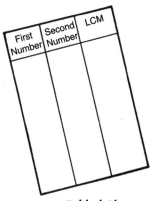

Three-Tab Venn Diagram

First Number	Second Number	LCM

Folded Chart

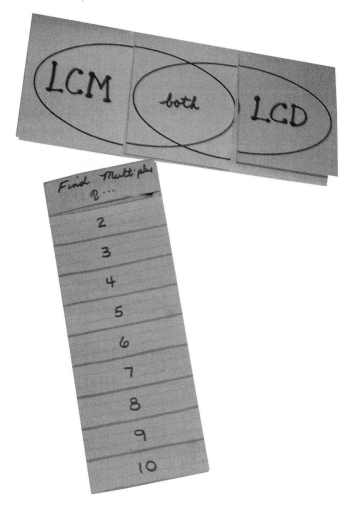

Monomials and Polynomials

Skill	Activity Suggestion	Foldable Parts
define	a monomial as an integer, a variable, or a product of integers and one or more variables	1
	a constant as a monomial that is a real number	1
Venn diagram	characteristics of monomials, constants, and both	3
list	ten examples of monomials and explain what they have in common	10
determine	whether an expression is or is not a monomial and explain your reasoning	2
multiply	monomials	any number
describe	in words and symbols the Power of a Monomial	2
Venn diagram	Power of a Product Property, Power of a Power Property, both = Power of a Monomial	3
divide	monomials	any number
explain	the degree of a monomial as the sum of the exponents of its variables	1
list	four monomials and their degrees	4
chart	examples of polynomials, or algebraic expressions, with one, two, three, and many terms	4
	examples of monomials, binomials, and trinomials	3
define	polynomial as a monomial, or a sum of monomials, and give four examples	4
find	the degree of three polynomials using the following: 1. find the degree of each term 2. determine the greatest degree of the terms 3. state the greatest degree of any term as the degree of the polynomial	3
add	polynomials and write about the process	any number
subtract	polynomials and write about the process	any number
find	the additive inverses of five polynomials	5
multiply	a polynomial by a monomial and outline the steps	2
simplify	four expressions involving polynomials	4
use	the FOIL method to multiply two binomials and the four steps	4

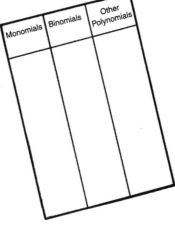

Folded Chart

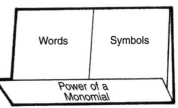

Two-Tab Matchbook

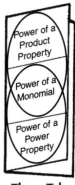

Three-Tab Venn Diagram

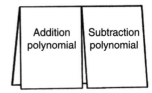

Two-Tab Book

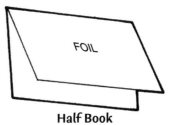

Half Book

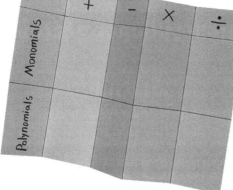

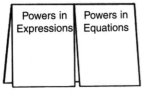

Two-Tab Book

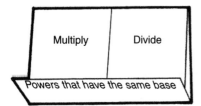

Two-Tab Matchbook

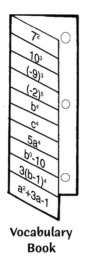

Vocabulary Book

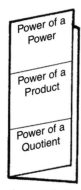

Three-Tab Book

Powers and Exponents

Skill	Activity Suggestion	Foldable Parts
define	powers as numbers that are expressed using exponents	1
read	expressions containing powers	any number
describe	how the second and third powers have special names related to geometry	2
write	expressions containing powers	any number
	expressions containing powers as multiplication expressions	any number
write	powers as multiplication expressions	any number
explain	how to multiply powers that have the same base	1
	how to divide powers that have the same base	1
compare and contrast	products of powers and quotients of powers	2
use	powers in expressions and equations	2
define	scientific notation as numbers written as the product of a factor and a power of 10	1
write	ten numbers using scientific notation	10
read	scientific notation	any number
order	numbers written in scientific notation	any number
compare	numbers in scientific notation with positive and negative exponents	2
use	scientific notation to evaluate five equations	5
outline	Properties of Powers—Power of a Power, Power of a Product, and Power of a Quotient	3
explain	how exponents are used to tell how many times a number is used as a factor	1
	rational exponents in words and symbols	2
define	the term base as it relates to exponents	1
write	four expressions using exponents	4
	three expressions with rational exponents in simplest radical form	3
evaluate	five expressions using exponents	5
show	expressions in either exponential or radical form	2
	numbers in standard and expanded form	2
use	the order of operations to evaluate algebraic expressions with powers	any number
write	expressions using positive and negative exponents	2
compare	the square of a difference and the square of a sum	2
tell	whether given expressions are in simplest form and why	2

Sequences

Skill	Activity Suggestion	Foldable Parts
define	an arithmetic sequence	1
explain	how to describe even and odd numbers as arithmetic sequences	2
differentiate between	numbers in a sequence and numbers in an arithmetic sequence	2
compare and contrast	sequences that are and are not arithmetic	2
describe	the terms of a sequence	1
find	the next terms of five given sequences	5
determine	the common differences of three arithmetic sequences	3
write	an original arithmetic sequence	1
outline	the steps you took to write an arithmetic sequence	
write	expressions that represent terms in a sequence	any number
research	the Fibonacci sequence and why the Fibonacci sequence is not arithmetic	2
define	a geometric sequence	1
explain	how each term in a geometric sequence increases or decreases by a common factor, called the common ratio	2
determine	if given sequences are geometric	2
find	the common ratio of a geometric sequence and list the next five terms	3

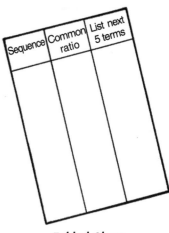

Folded Chart

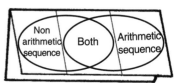

Three-Tab Venn Diagram

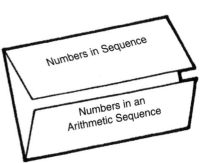

Shutter Fold

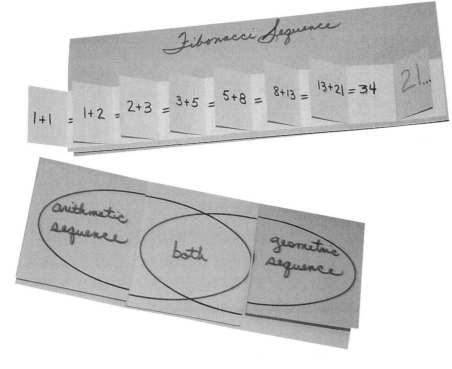

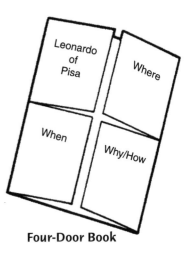

Four-Door Book

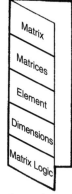

Five-Tab Book

Matrices

Skill	Activity Suggestion	Foldable Parts
define	matrix, matrices, element, dimensions, matrix logic	5
explain	how matrices organize data and give an example	2
give	two examples of square matrices	2
use	the singular word "matrix" and its plural form "matrices" correctly	2
compare and contrast	a matrix and a table	2
illustrate	how a matrix can be used to add, subtract, and multiply quantities	3
describe	how a matrix can be used to solve systems of equations with one, two, and three variables	3
research	the "what, where, when, why/how" of discrete mathematics	4
	Nine Chapters on the Mathematical Art, 250 B.C.	4
list	and explain algebraic rules for using matrices: scaler multiplication of a matrix, addition and subtraction of matrices, and multiplying matrices	any number
give	two examples of probability matrices	2
write	the identity matrices for three square matrices	3
find	the inverses of three 2×2 matrices	3
compare and contrast	the multiplicative inverse for real numbers to the inverse matrix	2

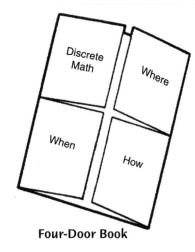

Four-Door Book

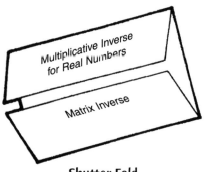

Shutter Fold

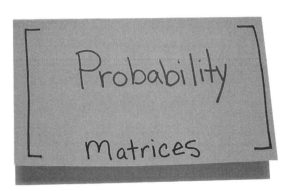

Points

Skill	Activity Suggestion	Foldable Parts
describe	a point as a specific location in space with no size or shape that is represented by a dot and named with a capital letter	1
identify	and model points and coplanar points	2
graph	eight ordered pairs on a coordinate plane	8
find	the distance between two points on a number line and two points in a coordinate plane	2
identify	how many end points a line, line segment, and a ray have	3

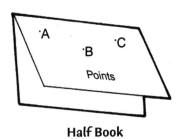

Half Book

Lines and Line Segments

Skill	Activity Suggestion	Foldable Parts
define	a line as a collection of points that extends in two directions, shown by arrowheads	1
list	two ways a line can be named	2
explain	a line segment as part of a line containing two endpoints and all of the points between	1
describe	how line segments are named	1
draw	and name five line segments	5
identify	and model lines that do and do not intersect	2
differentiate	between parallel lines and perpendicular lines	2
	between lines that intersect at a right angle and those that do not	2
illustrate	and explain a line called a *transversal*	2
find	the slopes of lines and use slope to identify parallel and perpendicular lines	2

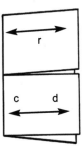

Two-Tab Book

Rays

Skill	Activity Suggestion	Foldable Parts
define	a ray as a portion of a line that extends from one point infinitely in one direction	1
describe	how a ray is named	1
Venn diagram	characteristics of a line segment, a ray, and both	3
illustrate	how two rays form and define an angle	2
compare and contrast	collinear and noncollinear rays	2

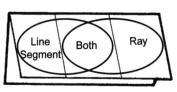

Three-Tab Venn Diagram

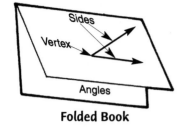

Folded Book

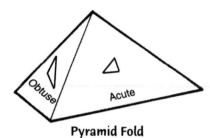

Pyramid Fold

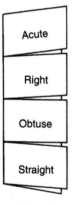

Four-Tab Book

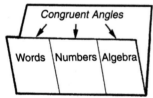

Three-Tab Concept Map

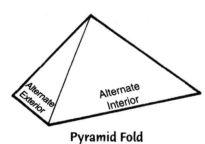

Pyramid Fold

Angles

Skill	Activity Suggestion	Foldable Parts
describe	an angle as two rays with the same endpoint	1
draw and label	the parts of an angle—vertex and sides	2
make	a concept map for "angles"	any number
summarize	and demonstrate how angles are measured and named	2
measure and name	ten angles using a protractor and report the measures in degrees	10
demonstrate	how a protractor can be used to draw an angle of a given measure	any number
differentiate	between acute, obtuse, and right angles	3
Venn diagram	characteristics of acute angles, obtuse angles, and both	3
classify	angles as acute, right, obtuse, or straight	4
explain	how an angle separates a plane into three parts: interior of the angle, exterior of the angle, and and the angle itself	3
draw	an angle that is congruent to a given angle	1
construct	the bisectors of four given angles	4

Angle Relationships

Skill	Activity Suggestion	Foldable Parts
justify	a straight line being called a "straight angle"	1
use	the term "transversal" when describing a line that intersects two parallel lines	1
draw	two intersecting lines and measure the angles formed	2
	parallel lines and measure the angles formed	2
	perpendicular lines and a transversal and explain why intersecting perpendicular lines form four right angles	2
show	rays and line segments can be perpendicular	2
describe	how the following are formed and give examples: vertical angles, adjacent angles, linear pair	3
differentiate	between complementary and supplementary angles	2
explain	alternate interior angles, alternate exterior angles, and corresponding angles	3
prove	that corresponding angles are congruent, alternate interior angles are congruent, and alternate exterior angles are congruent	3
compare and contrast	supplementary and complementary angles	2

Planes

Skill	Activity Suggestion	Foldable Parts
describe	a plane as a flat surface with no edges, or boundaries	1
explain	why lines in the same plane either intersect or are parallel	2
define	skew lines as two lines that do not intersect and are not in the same plane	1
draw	two examples of skew lines and explain why they are skew lines	2
find similarities and differences	between intersecting, parallel, and skew lines	2
Venn diagram	characteristics of parallel lines, skew lines, and both	3
illustrate	a rectangular prism and explain how it is formed by six planes	2
find	five examples of planes in your daily life	5
model	planes that do and do not intersect	2
write	five plane relationships and draw and label a figure for each	5
describe	and give four examples of coplanar points	5
compare	plane geometry and spherical geometry	2

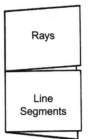

Two-Tab Book

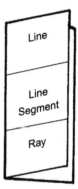

Three-Tab Book

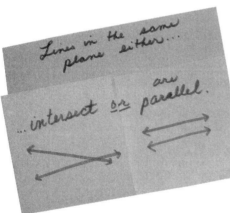

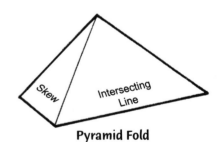

Pyramid Fold

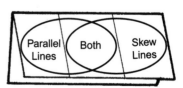

Three-Tab Venn Diagram

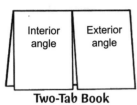

Two-Tab Book

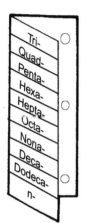

Vocabulary Book

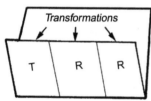

Three-Tab Concept Map

Six-Tab Book

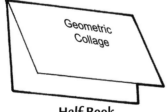

Half Book

Polygons

Skill	Activity Suggestion	Foldable Parts
define	polygons as simple closed figures in a plane formed by three or more line segments	1
classify	polygon as convex or concave	2
determine	the sum of the measures of the interior and exterior angles of a polygon	2
	how and why polygons are classified by their sides	2
explain	the meaning of the following prefixes—tri-, quad-, penta-,hexa-, hepta-, octa-, nona-, deca-, dodeca-, n-	9
draw and label	a triangle, a quadrilateral, a pentagon, a hexagon, an octagon, and a decagon	6
label	the vertices of the polygons you draw	any number
define	a diagonal as a line segment that joins two nonconsecutive vertices	1
explain	diagonals can not be drawn in a triangle, but can be drawn in any polygons with more than three sides	2
make a table	to show the number of sides, diagonals, and triangles formed in several different polygons—quadrilateral, pentagon, hexagon, heptagon, octagon	5
make a concept map	that shows a regular polygon is equilateral and equiangular	2
show	examples of interior and exterior angles of a polygon	2
differentiate between	polygons that are regular and polygons that are not regular	2
find	the sum of the measures of the interior angles of four different polygons heptagon = 900° nonagon = 1260° decagon = 1440° dodecagon = 1800°	4
make a table	to show the measures of the interior and exterior angles of three regular polygons	3
find	the perimeters of different polygons	any number
make a collage	of pictures of polygons	1
draw	a tessellation	1
determine	if three polygons will each tessellate	3
observe	tessellations in the form of quilts, fabric patterns, modern art, and more	any number
identify	regular and semi-regular (uniform) tessellations	2
define	transformations as movements of geometric figures	1
make a concept map	to show three types of transformations: translation, rotation, and reflection	3
draw	examples of translations, rotations, and reflections	3

Triangles

Skill	Activity Suggestion	Foldable Parts
define	a triangle as a three-sided polygon formed by three line segments that intersect only at their endpoints	1
	similarity of triangles as reflexive, symmetric, and transitive	3
	medians, altitudes, angle bisectors, and perpendicular bisectors	4
draw and label	a triangle and its vertices	2
name	triangles by their vertices	any number
find	the areas of three triangles	3
measure	the angles of four triangles	4
draw a conclusion	about the sum of the measures of the angles of all triangles	1
describe	the six types of triangles—acute, right, obtuse, equilateral, isosceles, and scalene	6
explain	how triangles are classified and classify four triangles by their angles and sides	4
draw and describe	two congruent triangles and their corresponding parts	2
make	a concept map on congruent triangles that explains how their corresponding sides are congruent and their corresponding angles are congruent	2
explain	how to find the area of a triangle in words and symbols	2
make a table	to define and give examples of the following: SSS, SAS, ASA, AAS	4
write	the Triangle Inequality Theorem and use it to show that some sets of line segments cannot be used to form triangles	2

Four-Tab Book

| Triangle |
| Quadrilateral |
| Pentagon |
| Hexagon |
| Heptagon |
| Octagon |

Six-Tab Book

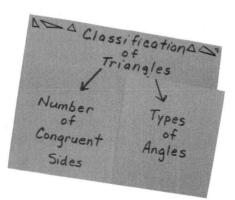

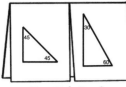

Two-Tab Book

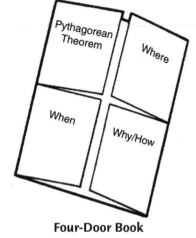

Four-Door Book

Right Triangles

Skill	Activity Suggestion	Foldable Parts
label	the parts of a right triangle—right angle, legs, hypotenuse	3
research	the history of the Pythagorean Theorem	4
explain	the Pythagorean Theorem in words and symbols	2
use	the Pythagorean Theorem to find the length of a side of a right triangle	1
determine	whether a triangle is a right triangle and explain your reasoning	2
describe	how to find the length of a leg of a right triangle if you know the lengths of the hypotenuse and the other leg	1
draw and label	a diagram to show the three altitudes of a right triangle	2
construct	right triangles from a square and form an equilateral triangle	2
compare and contrast	45°–45° right triangles, and 30°–60° right triangles	2
	tests for triangle congruence and tests for congruence of right triangles	2
illustrate	LL, HA, and LA as tests for congruence of right triangles	3

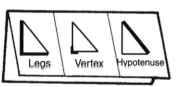

Three-Tab Book

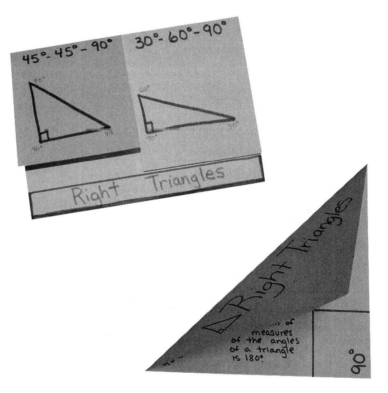

Right Triangle Trigonometry

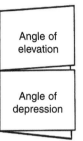

Two-Tab Book

Skill	Activity Suggestion	Foldable Parts
describe	trigonometry as the study of triangle properties and relationships	1
explain	the etymology of the word trigonometry	1
define	trigonometric ratios as the ratios of the measures of the sides of a right triangle	1
investigate	the following trigonometric ratios—sine, cosine, tangent ratios	3
report on	the trigonometic ratios sine, cosine, and tangent in words and symbols	3
compare and contrast	the sine ratio with the cosine ratio	2
tell	how to decide whether to use sine, cosine, or tangent when trying to measure an acute angle in a right triangle	3
describe	an angle of elevation and how it is formed by a horizontal line and a line of sight above it	2
show	an angle of depression and how it is formed by a horizontal line and a line of sight below it	2
draw	a diagram of an angle of elevation and an angle of depression	2
Venn diagram	characteristics of angle of elevation, an angle of depression, and both	3

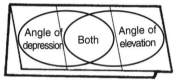

Three-Tab Venn Diagram

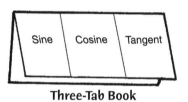

Three-Tab Book

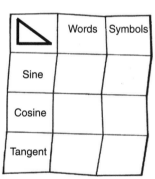

3 x 4 Folded Table

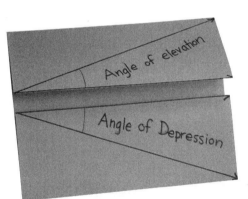

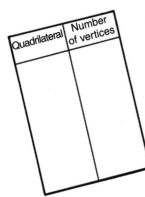

Folded Chart

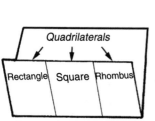

Six-Tab Book

Quadrilaterals

Skill	Activity Suggestion	Foldable Parts
define	a quadrilateral as a closed figure formed by four line segments that intersect only at their endpoints	1
draw and label	a quadrilateral and its vertices	2
compare and contrast	a quadrilateral and a non-example of a quadrilateral	2
measure	the angles of several quadrilaterals	any number
draw a conclusion	about the sum of the measures of the angles of a quadrilateral	1
explain	how quadrilaterals can be classified	1
describe	six types of quadrilaterals: 1. quadrilaterals with no pairs of parallel lines 2. parallelogram = quadrilateral with two pairs of parallel sides 3. trapezoid = quadrilateral with exactly one pair of parallel sides 4. rectangle = parallelogram with four congruent angles 5. square = parallelogram with congruent sides and congruent angles 6. rhombus = parallelogram with congruent sides	6
make a concept map	that shows the six types of quadrilaterals	6
illustrate	different quadrilaterals and their diagonals	any number

Three-Tab Concept Map

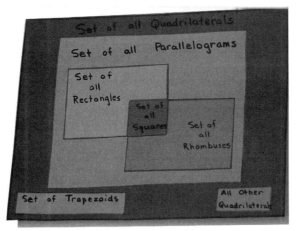

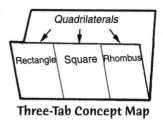

Three-Tab Concept Map

Squares, Rectangles, and Rhombi

Skill	Activity Suggestion	Foldable Parts
describe	a square and a rectangle in words and symbols	2
Venn diagram	characteristics of a square, a rectangle, and both	3
describe	and illustrate two different quadrilaterals with four right angles—a square and a rectangle	2
find	the perimeters of rectangles, squares, and rhombi	3
	the areas of rectangles, squares, and rhombi	3
describe	equilateral and equiangular figures	2
draw	a square and a rectangle with the same area on grid paper	2
illustrate	the diagonals of squares and rectangles	2
make a table	to compare and contrast the following characteristics of squares and rectangles: • are diagonals congruent? • are pairs of opposite sides congruent? • are diagonals perpendicular? • is one pair of opposite sides parallel and congruent?	any number
summarize	and diagram the properties of a rectangle: • opposite sides are congruent and parallel • opposite angles are congruent • consecutive angles are supplementary • diagonals are congruent and bisect each other • all four angles are right angles	5
compare and contrast	squares and rhombi	2
diagram	the diagonals of a rhombus and prove that they are perpendicular	2
	the diagonals of a rhombus and show how they bisect opposite angles	2
Venn diagram	characteristics of rhombi, rectangles, and both	3

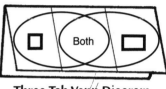

Two-Tab Book

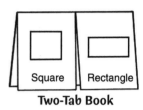

Three-Tab Venn Diagram

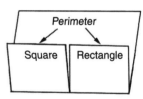

Two-Tab Concept Map

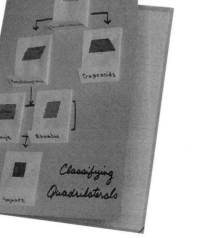

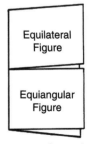

Two-Tab Book

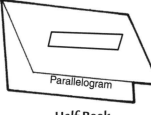

Half Book

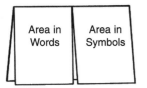

Two-Tab Book

Parallelograms

Skill	Activity Suggestion	Foldable Parts
define	a parallelogram as a four-sided figure with both pairs of opposite sides parallel	1
draw	an example of a parallelogram	1
find similarities	between a general quadrilateral and a parallelogram	2
label	the base and the height of a parallelogram	2
find	the area of given parallelogram by multiplying the measures of the base and the height	any number
illustrate	a parallelogram and show its diagonals	2
describe	how to find the area of a parallelogram in words and in symbols	2
diagram	and explain the following five properties of parallelograms: • opposite sides are parallel • opposite sides are congruent • opposite angles are congruent • consecutive angles are supplementary • the diagonals bisect each other	5
use	the properties above to test four quadrilaterals to determine if they are parallelograms	4
write	a two-column proof and a paragraph proof for the following theorem: If one pair of opposite sides of a quadrilateral are parallel and congruent, then the quadrilateral is a parallelogram.	2
prove	that a quadrilateral with four congruent sides is a parallelogram	1
Venn diagram	characteristics of a rhombus, a parallelogram, and both	3

Five-Tab Book

Property 1

Property 2

Property 3

Property 4

Property 5

Three-Tab Venn Diagram

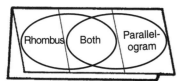

Trapezoids

Skill	Activity Suggestion	Foldable Parts
define	a trapezoid as a quadrilateral with exactly two parallel sides called bases	1
draw	a trapezoid and label the bases, legs, and height or the altitude	2
explain	how you can use triangles to find the area of different trapezoids	any number
describe	how to find the area of a trapezoid in words and symbols	2
compare and contrast	the altitude of a triangle and the altitude of a trapezoid	2
draw	a parallelogram, a triangle, and a trapezoid with the same area on grid paper	3
illustrate	the diagonals in given trapezoids	any number
construct	the median of a trapezoid and outline the steps	2
compare	an isosceles triangle and an isosceles trapezoid	2
Venn diagram	characteristics of an isosceles trapezoid, a non-isosceles trapezoid, and both	3
recognize	the properties of trapezoids: • the bases are parallel • the median is parallel to the bases and its measure is half of the sum of the measures of the bases	2

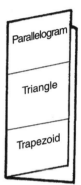

Two-Tab Book

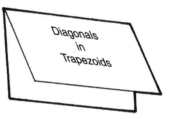

Three-Tab Book

Half Book

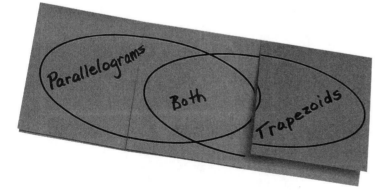

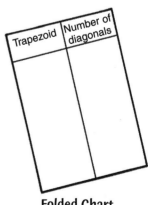

Folded Chart

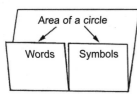

Two-Tab Concept Map

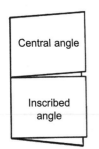

Two-Tab Book

Half Book

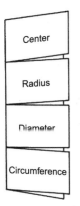

Four-Tab Book

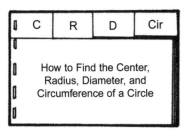

Top-Tab Book

Circles

Skill	Activity Suggestion	Foldable Parts
use	a compass to draw circles	any number
define	center, radius, diameter, and circumference	4
label	the center, radius, diameter, and circumference of a circle	4
explain	how to find the radius of a circle if the diameter is known	any number
draw	three circles on grid paper and estimate their areas by counting grid squares	3
find	the circumference of a circle if given the radius and find the circumference given the diameter	2
	the area of a circle	any number
describe	in words and symbols how to find the area of a circle	2
explain	how to find the area of a circle if you know the measure of the radius	1
investigate	the history of and the use of pi, or 3.14159...	2
explain	why pi is not a rational number and give rational numbers that could be used as approximations for pi	2
illustrate	three chords of a circle	3
describe	the diameter of a circle as the longest chord that can be drawn and illustrate	2
illustrate	a central angle of a circle and describe it as an angle whose vertex is the center of a circle	2
label and measure	a central angle and the major and minor arcs it intercepts	2
compare and contrast	a central angle and an inscribed angle	2
use a compass	to draw a semicircle	1
differentiate	between concentric circles and congruent circles	2
	chords, tangents, and secents	2
recognize	tangents and use properties of tangents	2

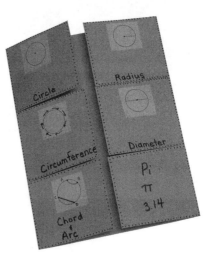

Three-Dimensional Figures

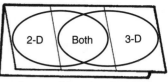

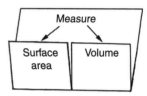

Three-Tab Venn Diagram

Skill	Activity Suggestion	Foldable Parts
identify	three-dimensional figures	any number
Venn diagram	characteristics of two-dimensional figures, three-dimensional figures, and both	3
explain	surface area and volume as they relate to three-dimensional figures	2
list	examples of ways in which you use surface area and volume in your daily life	2
describe	how surface area is measured by square units and volume is measured in cubic units	2
use	top, front, side, and corner views of three-dimensional solids to make models	
draw	pyramids, cones, cylinders, and prisms	4
define	polyhedron and give three examples	3
illustrate	the five types of regular polyhedra, also called the Platonic solids	5
name	the edges, faces, and vertices of polyhedrons you draw	any number

Two-Tab Concept Map

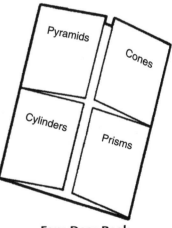

Four-Door Book

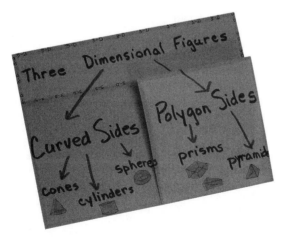

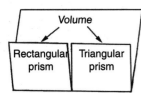

Two-Tab Concept Map

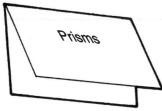

Half Book

Two-Tab Book

Prisms and Cylinders

Skill	Activity Suggestion	Foldable Parts
define	prism as a solid figure that has two parallel congruent sides, called bases	1
explain	why you think prisms are named by the shape of their bases	1
draw	examples of rectangular prisms and triangular prisms	2
show	the nets of a rectangular and a triangular prism	2
find	the surface area of a rectangular prism	1
find	the surface area of a triangular prism	1
find	the volumes of a rectangular prism and a triangular prism	2
describe	in words and symbols how to find the volume of a prism	2
list	examples of prisms you encounter in your daily life	any number
define	cylinder as a three-dimensional shape with two parallel, congruent, circular bases	1
draw	a cylinder and label the bases and an altitude	2
list	examples of cylinders you encounter in a week's time	any number
show	the net of a cylinder	1
find	the surface area of a cylinder	1
find	the volume of a cylinder	1
describe	in words and symbols how to find the volume of a cylinder	2
Venn diagram	method for finding the volume of a prism, the volume of a cylinder, and both	3

Pyramids and Cones

Skill	Activity Suggestion	Foldable Parts
define	pyramid as a solid figure that has a polygon for a base	1
explain	why you think pyramids are named by their bases	1
compare and contrast	a square pyramid and a triangular pyramid	2
describe	a pyramid's base, lateral faces, and vertex	3
illustrate	a pyramid's slant height and a pyramid's net	2
find	the surface area of a rectangular or triangular pyramid	1
	the volume of a rectangular or triangular pyramid	1
describe	in words and symbols how to find the volume of a pyramid	2
define	cone as a three-dimensional shape with a circular base and one vertex	1
show	the slant height and the net of a cone	2
explain	in your own words how to find the surface areas of a cone and a pyramid	2
describe	in words and symbols how to find the volume of a cone	2
Venn diagram	characteristics of a cone, a pyramid, and both	3

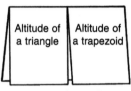

Shutter Fold

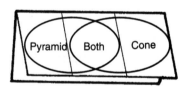

Two-Tab Book

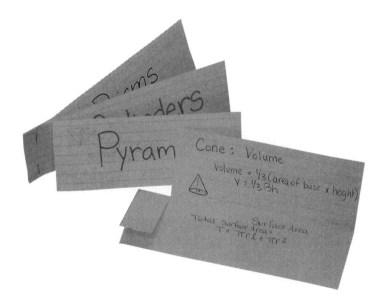

Three-Tab Venn Diagram

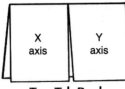

Two-Tab Book

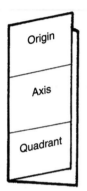

Three-Tab Book

Coordinate Geometry

Skill	Activity Suggestion	Foldable Parts
describe	a coordinate system as the intersection of two number lines that meet at their zero points	1
explain	how a point can be located using a coordinate system	1
define	origin as the intersection point of two number lines at their zero points	1
differentiate between	the *x*-axis and the *y*-axis	2
draw	a coordinate system and label the origin, *x*-axis, and *y*-axis	2
describe	how to use an ordered pair to graph a point on a coordinate system	1
mark and name	points on a grid	any number
name	the ordered pairs for given points a grid	any number
find	examples of coordinate systems used in your daily life	any number
Venn diagram	characteristics of latitude lines, longitude lines, and both	3
describe	how the two axes of a coordinate system to divide the coordinate plane into four regions called quadrants	4
draw	a coordinate system and label the origin, axes, and quadrants	3
explain	what it means to graph or plot a point	1
plot	points such as (5, 7) and (7, 5) and explain how they differ	any number
graph	points on a coordinate plane and name them	any number

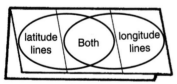

Three-Tab Venn Diagram

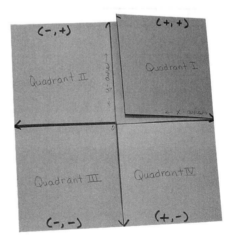

Slope

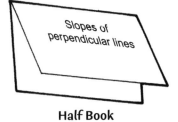

Two-Tab Concept Map

Skill	Activity Suggestion	Foldable Parts
define	the slope of a line	1
differentiate between	the vertical change, or the change in y, and the horizontal change, or the change in x	2
find	the slope of a line when given two points on the line	any number
explain	in words and symbols how to find the slope of a line	2
illustrate	the rise (vertical change) and the run (horizontal change) of a line	2
describe	slope as "rise over run"	1
define	parallel lines as lines that will never intersect	1
explain	the relationship between the slopes of parallel lines	1
make a conjecture	about the slopes of perpendicular lines	1

Two-Tab Book

Half Book

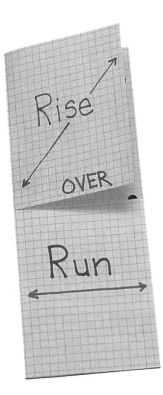

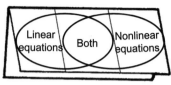

Three-Tab Venn Diagram

Graphing Equations and Inequalities

Skill	Activity Suggestion	Foldable Parts
graph	linear equations in two variables	any number
find	the x- and y-intercepts of graphs	any number
graph	linear equations using the x- and y-intercepts	any number
Venn diagram	characteristics of linear equations, nonlinear equations, and both	3
compare and contrast	quadratic equations and cubic equations	2
explore	the characteristics of slope	1
find	the slope of a line given its equation	any number
investigate	rate of change	1
graph	linear inequalities	any number
define	parabola	1
illustrate	the graph of a parabola	1
use	tables and graphs to write linear functions	2
define	inequalities	1
explain	how to graph inequalities	1

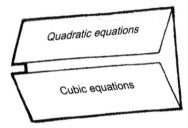

Shutter Fold

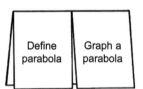

Two-Tab Book

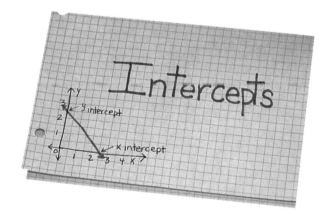

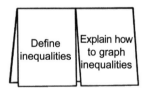

Two-Tab book

Metric Measurement

Skill	Activity Suggestion	Foldable Parts
investigate	the development of the metric system of measurement by French scientists in 1795	1
define	a meter (m) as $\frac{1}{10,000,000}$ of the distance between the North Pole and the Equator	1
chart	the prefixes used with the metric system	any number
note	each place value is 10 times the place value to its right	any number
make	a place value chart for the metric system	any number
convert	measurements within the metric system	any number
	Customary units to metric units	any number

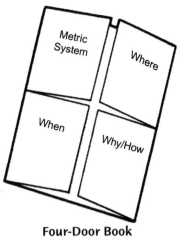

Four-Door Book

Length, Width, and Height

Skill	Activity Suggestion	Foldable Parts
research	the history of the measurement of length, width, and height	3
explain	inches, feet, yards	3
	millimeters, centimeters, meters	3
write	word problems based upon length and width	any number
	measurments in numbers and words	any number
read	Customary and metric measurements of length and width	2
	instruments used to record length, width, and height	any number
record	common uses of length and width	any number

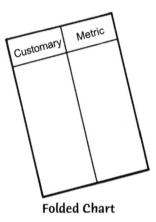

Folded Chart

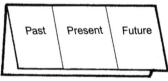

Three-Tab Book

Distance

Half Book

Skill	Activity Suggestion	Foldable Parts
define	distance as the space between two points or locations	1
research	the history of the measurement of distance	any number
explain	inches, feet, yards, miles	4
	centimeters, meters, kilometers	3
write	word problems based upon distance	any number
read	instruments used to measure distance	any number
investigate	light-years and explain how and why this unit of measurement was developed	2
	astronomical units (AU)	1
	microns, or millionths of a meter, and millimicrons, or thousandths of a micron	2

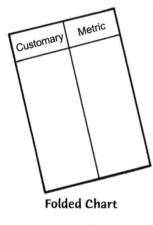

Folded Chart

Weight

Skill	Activity Suggestion	Foldable Parts
define	weight as the gravitational force, or pull, on an object	1
explain	why objects have no weight in space	1
	why objects on a planet smaller than Earth would weigh less than they do on Earth	1
investigate	common units of weight measurement: ounce/pound and gram/kilogram	2
estimate	weight based upon experiences	any number

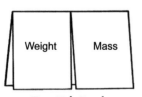

Two-Tab Book

Volume

Skill	Activity Suggestion	Foldable Parts
define	volume as the amount of space something occupies	1
compare and contrast	the measurement of volume of a solid and a liquid	2
find	the volume of two rectangular solids by using the formula $V = \ell wh$	2
	the volume of a cylinder using the formula $V = \pi r^2 h$	1
	the volume of a sphere using the formula $V = \frac{4}{3}\pi r^3$	1
evaluate	the number of cubic inches in a cubic foot and the number of cubic centimeters in a cubic meter	2
describe	how liquids are measured in the customary system and in the metric system	2
use	gallons, quarts, pints, and fluid ounces	4
	liters and milliliters	2

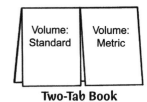

Two-Tab Book

Temperature

Skill	Activity Suggestion	Foldable Parts
research	the history of the measurement of temperature	any number
write	three word problems based upon temperature	3
read	and report metric and customary system measurements of temperature	2
differentiate	between degrees Celsius and degrees Fahrenheit	2
research and graph	the average body temperatures of five animals	5
make a table	of average air temperatures of different geographic regions or areas	any number
	of average surface and core temperatures of the planets in our solar system	2
record	temperatures at predetermined intervals over a given period of time	2
read	instruments used to measure temperature	any number
investigate	the International Temperature Scale of 1990	1
	Kelvin, K, the unit of thermodynamic temperature	1
	absolute zero, $-273.15°C$ or $-459.67°F$	1

Three-Tab Book

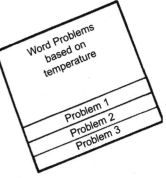

Layered-Look Book (2 sheets of paper)

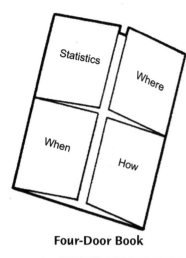

Four-Door Book

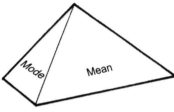

Pyramid Fold

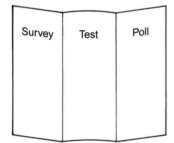

Trifold Book

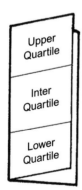

Three-Tab Book

Statistics

Skill	Activity Suggestion	Foldable Parts
define	statistics as a branch of mathematics that involves collecting and presenting data	1
describe	ways in which statisticians collect and present data	2
define	mean, median, and mode individually and collectively as measures of central tendency of a set of data	3
analyze	data using mean, median, and mode	3
find	the mean and median for a set of data	2
explain	the range of a set of numbers	1
determine	the range of a set of data	any number
separate	a large set of data into four equal parts, or quartiles	4
illustrate	how the median of a set of data divides the data in half	2
write	the definition of interquartile range in words and symbols	2
sequence	the steps for finding the range and interquartile range of a set of data. 1. List the data from least to greatest. 2. Find the median. 3. Find the upper quartile, or the median of the upper half. 4. Find the lower quartile, or the median of the lower half. 5. Find the interquartile range by subtracting the upper quartile range from the lower quartile range.	5
use	measures of variation to compare data	any number
list	ways in which measures of variation are used in everyday life or in a work place	any number
find	the range, median, upper quartile, lower quartile, and the interquartile range for sets of data	5
describe	how statistics are used in written and oral communication to prove points and influence opinions	2
explain	ways in which statistics might be misleading	any number
recognize	and find examples of misleading statistics	any number
find	examples of graphs in a newspaper or magazine, determine if they are or are not misleading, and explain why or why not	2
list	things you might question when reading the results of a survey, test, or poll	any number
use	the same data with two different scales and explain how these graphs look different	2

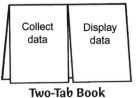

Two-Tab Book

Stem-and-Leaf Plots

Skill	Activity Suggestion	Foldable Parts
describe	a stem-and-leaf plot	1
define	the stem and leaf	2
illustrate	how to organize data into stems and leaves	2
explain	the purposes of the "stem" and the "leaf"	2
show	how data values with numerous digits can be rounded so that each leaf has only one digit	1
collect	data that can be organized into a stem-and-leaf plot, such as student grades on a test	any number
display	data in stem-and-leaf plots	any number
sequence	the steps used for making a stem-and-leaf plot	any number
interpret	data presented in stem-and-leaf plots made by classmates	any number
compare and contrast	a regular stem-and-leaf plot and a back-to-back stem-and-leaf plot	2
make	a back-to-back stem-and-leaf plot	1
Venn Diagram	charactertistics a stem-and-leaf plot, a bar graph, and both	3

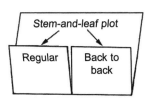

Two-Tab Concept Map

Three-Tab Venn Diagram

Box-and-Whisker Plots

Skill	Activity Suggestion	Foldable Parts
define	quartiles and extreme values of a set of data as each relate to a box-and-whisker plot	2
display	data in box-and-whisker plots	any number
explain	the purpose for using box-and-whisker plots and describe how they present important characteristics of data visually	1
sequence	the steps for constructing a box-and-whisker plot. 1. Draw a number line for the range of the data. 2. Above the number line, mark points for the upper and lower extremes, the median, and the upper and lower quartile values. 3. Draw a box that contains the quartile values. 4. Draw a vertical line through the median value. 5. Extend the whiskers from each quartile to the upper and lower extreme data points.	5
list	five things that can be learned from a box-and-whisker plot	5
define	outliers as data that are more than 1.5 times the interquartile range from the quartiles	1
Venn Diagram	characteristics of a box-and-whisker plot, a stem-and-leaf plot, and both	3

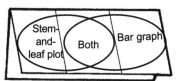

Three-Tab Venn Diagram

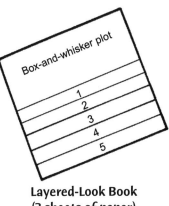

**Layered-Look Book
(3 sheets of paper)**

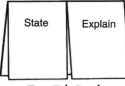

Two-Tab Book

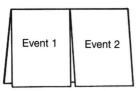

Two-Tab Book

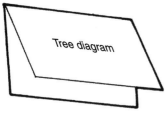

Half Book

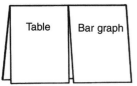

Two-Tab Book

Fundamental Counting Principle

Skill	Activity Suggestion	Foldable Parts
explain	the Fundamental Counting Principle	1
draw	a tree diagram to show the possible outcomes for two events, such as tossing a dime and then tossing a nickel, and explain your drawing	2
describe	independent events and dependent events as they relate to the Fundamental Counting Principle	2

Frequency Tables

Skill	Activity Suggestion	Foldable Parts
describe	the purpose of a frequency table	1
differentiate between	a frequency table and a bar graph	2
explain	why a frequency table is good when you want to know specific numbers	1

Pascal's Triangle

Skill	Activity Suggestion	Foldable Parts
define	the following terms as they relate to Pascal's triangle: expand powers, binomials, binomial theorem, exponents, coefficients	5
explain	Pascal's triangle in your own words	1
	the Binomial Theorem in your own words	1
describe	how to form two additional rows of Pascal's triangle	2
research	the "who, what, where, when" of: Blaise Pascal and Pascal's triangle	4
	Sir Isaac Newton and his discovery of ways in which the Binomial Theorem can lead to an infinite series	4
make a timeline	of the history of this triangle	any number

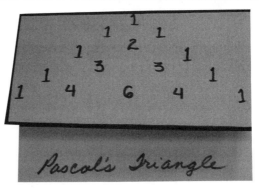

Permutations

Skill	Activity Suggestion	Foldable Parts
define	permutation as an arrangement or listing in which order is important	1
use	the symbol $P(6, 3)$ to represent the number of permutations of 6 things taken 3 at a time	1
find	values for problems such as $P(5, 5)$ and make models to illustrate their meaning	2
observe	two ways in which you might use permutations in your daily life	2
list	three examples of permutations	3
write	four permutations as word problems	4
differentiate	between linear permutations and circular permutations	2
explain	the rule for permutations with repetitions in writing and give an example	2
determine	whether something is a combination or a permutation	2

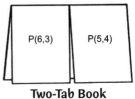

Two-Tab Book

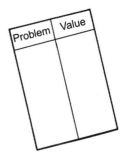

Folded Chart

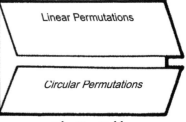

Shutter Fold

Combinations

Skill	Activity Suggestion	Foldable Parts
differentiate between	permutations and combinations	2
summarize	the difference between a permutation and a combination of 3 things taken 2 at a time	2
draw	models to illustrate two combinations	2
define	combinations as arrangements or listings where order is not important	1
use	the symbol $C(6, 3)$ to represent the number of combinations of 6 things taken 3 at a time	any number
observe	ways in which you might use combinations in your daily life	any number
list	examples of combinations	any number
find	values for problems such as $C(5, 4)$	any number
write	word problems involving combinations	any number

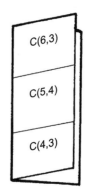

Three-Tab Book

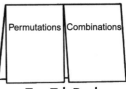

Two-Tab Book

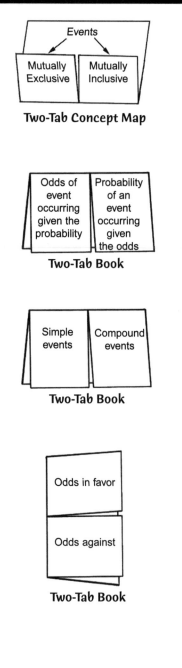

Events

Mutually Exclusive | Mutually Inclusive

Two-Tab Concept Map

Odds of event occurring given the probability | Probability of an event occurring given the odds

Two-Tab Book

Simple events | Compound events

Two-Tab Book

Odds in favor

Odds against

Two-Tab Book

Probability

Skill	Activity Suggestion	Foldable Parts
define	probability as the chance that some event will happen	1
describe	probability as the ratio of the number of ways a certain event can occur to the number of possible outcomes	1
explain	the set of all possible outcomes as the sample space	1
find	the probability of three simple events	3
	the probability of two compound events	2
describe	the probability of two independent events in words and symbols	2
	the probability of two dependent events in words and symbols	2
define	the term *odds* as a way to describe the chance of an event occurring	1
explain	odds in favor and odds against	2
	probability of success and failure	2
differentiate	between probability and odds	2
give	examples of mutually exclusive events	any number
describe	how to find the probability of mutually exclusive events in words and symbols	2
define	inclusive events and give two examples	2
describe	how to find the probability of inclusive events in words and symbols	2
compare and contrast	mutually exclusive and inclusive events	2
	dependent and independent events	2
make	a vocabulary book for the following terms: dependent events, experimental probability, inclusive, independent events, mutually exclusive, odds, relative frequency, simulation	8
state	the odds of an event occurring given the probability and the probability of an event occurring given the odds	2

Scatter Plots

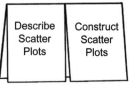

Two-Tab Book

Skill	Activity Suggestion	Foldable Parts
define	a scatter plot as a graph that shows the general relationship between two sets of data	1
construct	scatter plots	any number
interpret	scatter plots	any number
differentiate between	scatter plots that show a positive relationship, negative relationship, and no relationship	3
write	about three ways in which scatter plots might be used: display data, examine trends, make predictions	3
describe	how to draw a scatter plot for two sets of data	1
create	a scatter plot to analyze data	1
draw	lines of fit for sets of data on a scatter plot	1
use	lines of fit to make predictions about data	1
define	and determine a prediction equation	2

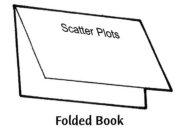

Folded Book

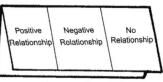

Three-Tab Book

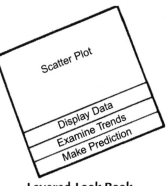

Layered-Look Book (2 sheets of paper)

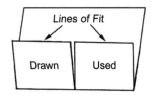

Two-Tab Concept Map

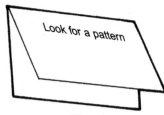

Half Book

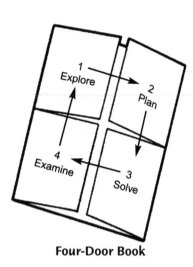

Four-Door Book

Problem-Solving Plan

Skill	Activity Suggestion	Foldable Parts
describe	the four steps of the problem-solving plan in writing	4
solve	problems using the four-step problem-solving plan	any number
explain	how the four-step plan gives you an organized method for solving problems	1
demonstrate	how to use the problem-solving plan	1
choose	appropriate methods of computation when using the problem-solving plan	4
describe	how looking for a pattern is a good problem-solving technique	1

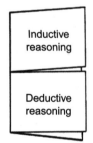

Four-Tab Book

Problem-Solving Strategies

Skill	Activity Suggestion	Foldable Parts
give	three examples of inductive reasoning	3
	three examples of deductive reasoning	3
compare and contrast	inductive and deductive reasoning	2

Two-Tab Book

Folded Chart

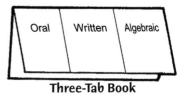

Three-Tab Book

Vocabulary and Writing Definitions

Skill	Activity Suggestion	Foldable Parts
explain	the meaning of a word or process in your own words	1
define	terms by giving written examples	any number
	terms orally, in writing, and algebraically	3
write	the definition of terms concisely	any number
	a descriptive paragraph using the vocabulary words and concepts introduced in a lesson	1
use	vocabulary words in your speech and writing as frequently as possible	any number
	a dictionary to find definitions of your math vocabulary words and compare the dictionary definition to the defintion given in your textbook	2
	the Internet to find definitions and examples of properties, or functions	3
self-check	your knowledge of terms and concepts by observing a word and mentally defining it	any number
quiz	friends and family members to see if they know the meaning of your vocabulary words	any number

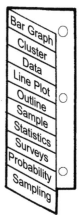

Vocabulary Book

Journals

Skill	Activity Suggestion	Foldable Parts
explain	descriptively what you are learning	1
define	terms, concepts, properties, and more in your math journal	any number
write	about personal associations and experiences called to mind during the learning process	any number
evaluate	the direction and progress of your learning in your journal	1
list	examples of ways in which new knowledge has or will be used in daily life experiences	any number
read	journal notes of fellow students and compare their experiences with your own	2
describe	positive and negative experiences during your learning process	2
use	journals for self-questioning by recording questions that arise during learning	any number
	journals to organize thinking by including sketches, diagrams, and examples	any number

Bound Book

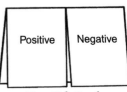

Two-Tab Book

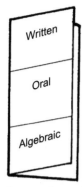

Three-Tab Book

Outline, List, and Sequence

Skill	Activity Suggestion	Foldable Parts
note	the order in which concepts are presented in lessons and texts	1
explain	why certain concepts are presented in a specific sequence	1
	why there is an order of operations	1
describe	an order of operations as a sequence and describe its importance	2
outline	the steps used to solve given problems	any number
	how several students reached a solution and compare and contrast the outlines	any number
	the main ideas and supporting facts presented in a lesson or chapter	any number
list	examples of specific things studied, such as operations, processes, properties, and more	any number

Concept Map

Concept Maps

Skill	Activity Suggestion	Foldable Parts
explain	the use of a concept map	1
design	a concept map to organize information presented in a lesson or text chapter	any number
use	a concept map as a study guide to review main ideas and supporting information	any number

Half Book

Writing Instructions

Skill	Activity Suggestion	Foldable Parts
explain	the importance of writing clear, concise instructions	1
write	a set of instructions on how to do something presented in a lesson	any number
ask	students to follow their own instructions to check them for accuracy and clarity	2
	students to follow instructions written by classmates to check them for accuracy and clarity	2

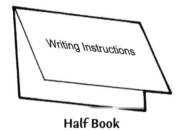

Layered-Look Book

Main Ideas and Note Taking

Skill	Activity Suggestion	Foldable Parts
determine	main ideas	any number
outline	main ideas and supporting information or facts	any number
describe	note taking as a skill that is based upon listening or reading for main ideas and then recording these ideas for future reference	1
use	a journal to take notes on a specific topic	any number
	a concept map to record a main idea and supporting facts	any number

Bound Book

Annotations

Skill	Activity Suggestion	Foldable Parts
write	annotations or notes to organize the text they are reading for review or study	any number
	annotations that include the following: key points highlighted or copied into a journal reader questions that arise reader comments reader reactions to text short summaries steps or data numbered by reader	any number

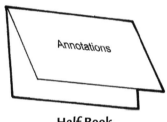

Half Book

Questioning

Skill	Activity Suggestion	Foldable Parts
note	different ways in which questioning is used in the learning process	any number
develop	the skill of self questioning during learning	2
write	personal questions that arise during learning	1
practice	asking questions in a clear and concise manner	any number
differentiate	between questions that can be answered using *yes* or *no* responses to those that are open ended	2
find	examples of the following: questions without answers questions that have only one answer questions with multiple answers	3
formulate	questions that can be addressed with data and collect, organize, and display data to answer the questions	any number

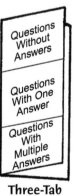

Three-Tab Book

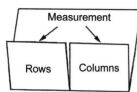

Concept Map

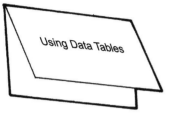

Half Book

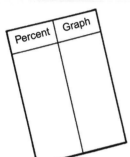

Folded Chart

Bound Book

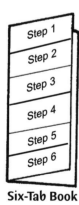

Six-Tab Book

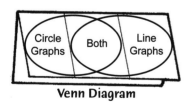

Venn Diagram

Tables and Charts

Skill	Activity Suggestion	Foldable Parts
chart	information using rows or columns	any number
describe	a data table as having rows and columns	1
	the importance of labeling the title of a data table and labeling the rows and columns	1
make	a data table	any number
outline	steps taken to make a specific data table	any number
write	information in the appropriate columns and rows of a data table	any number
use	data collected in a table to write a summary	1

Circle Graphs

Skill	Activity Suggestion	Foldable Parts
explain	how circle graphs show the parts of something as they relate to the whole	1
	why circle graphs are also called pie graphs or pie charts	1
make and label	a circle graph based upon data expressed as percents	2
	a circle graph based upon data that is not expressed as percents	2
convert	data into percents and report it using a circle graph	any number
describe	each section of a circle graph as a segment of the circle	2
use	a protractor to measure the central angles of three circle graphs	1
	a protractor to draw the central angles of three circle graphs	1
sequence	the steps for converting data into percents so it can be presented using a circle graph	6
Venn diagram	characteristics of circle graphs, bar graphs, and both	3

Bar Graphs and Histograms

Skill	Activity Suggestion	Foldable Parts
describe	a histogram as a bar graph that shows the frequency distribution of data	1
make and label	a bar graph	2
	a histogram	2
explain	single and double bar graphs	2
define	a double bar graph as a comparative graph	1
explain	how a double bar graph can be used to show trends	1
make and label	a double bar graph	2
use	a bar graph to compare increases and decreases in quantity over a period of time	2
collect	examples of bar graphs encountered in daily life	any number

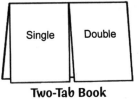

Two-Tab Book

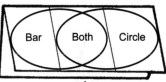

Half Book

Line Graphs

Skill	Activity Suggestion	Foldable Parts
explain	how line graphs can be used to show how values change over a period of time	1
use	line graphs to compare numbers	any number
	line graphs to show trends or patterns	any number
develop	a grid and make your own line graph	1
label	and explain the vertical and horizontal axes of your line graph	2
describe	which axis shows frequency and which shows categories	2
	what the points on a line graph indicate and explain why straight lines are used to connect the points	2
make and label	line graphs to show the following: • student grades over a period of time • production level or sales over time • population of an area over time • income over time	2

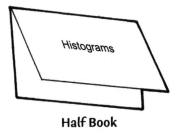

Venn Diagram

Bound Book

Two-Tab Book

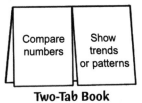

Matchbook

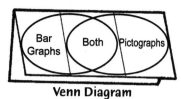

Venn Diagram

Bound Book

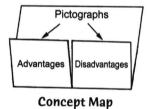

Concept Map

Pictographs

Skill	Activity Suggestion	Foldable Parts
explain	how pictographs use pictures or symbols to show how specific quantities compare	1
make and label	a pictograph and determine what value each symbol will represent	2
research	the historic origins of pictographs	4
compare and contrast	pictographs and bar graphs	2
collect	examples of pictographs and explain their use	any number
list	advantages and disadvantages of using pictographs	2
note	where and how pictographs are used	2

Venn Diagrams

Skill	Activity Suggestion	Foldable Parts
explain	how a Venn diagram can be used to display data and show how the data is related	2
	how a Venn diagram can be used to find similarities in data	1
describe	the purpose of a rectangle, circles, and the space formed by overlapping circles in a Venn diagram	3
differentiate between	using a two circle and a three circle Venn diagram	2
make	a Venn diagram to display given data and outline the procedure you used	2
compare and contrast	data presented in a Venn diagram	2
use	Venn diagrams to illustrate two conditional statements	2
write	three conditional statements based upon data illustrated by a Venn diagram: If_____, then_____.	3
draw	a Venn diagram to illustrate data and write four true statements	4

Using Visuals and Graphics with Foldables

I designed the graphics on pages 94–111 to be used as visual aids for student production, while immersing students in measurement, percentages, maps, and time lines. At times, I require these graphics to be used in student presentations. I photocopy them or print them from my computer and pass them out. At other times, students incorporate them into their journals, notes, projects, and study guides independently. I found that students and teachers were more likely to use graphics if they were available on a classroom computer where they could be selected and printed out as needed.

1. Mark and label large world map to show where past and recent events in mathematics occurred or where a historic or modern mathematician lived and worked.

2. Mark and label smaller maps of continents to illustrate more specific locations, for example, when making a "who, what, when, where" Foldable.

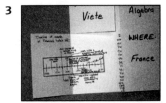

3. Use time lines to record when a mathematician lived or when an event or sequence of events occurred. Use two time lines to compare what was happening in two different areas at the same time.

4. Use small picture frames to sketch or name a person, place, or thing. Great to use with the four-door book as a "who, what, when, where" activity.

   NOTE: *I grant you permission to photocopy or electronically scan these pages (94-111) and place copies of them in the production center or publishing center of your classroom.*

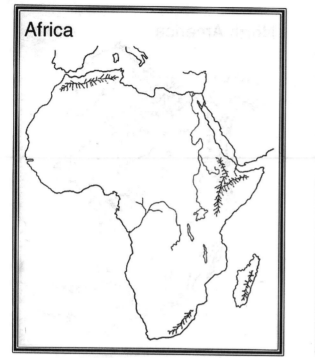

Africa

Antarctica

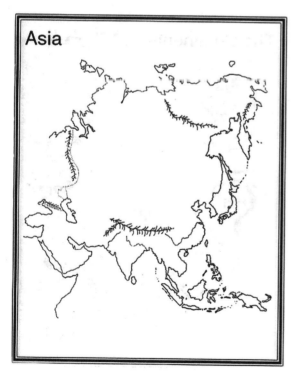

Asia

Australia

Europe

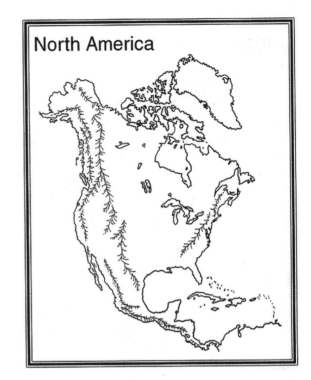

North America

South America

Picture Frame

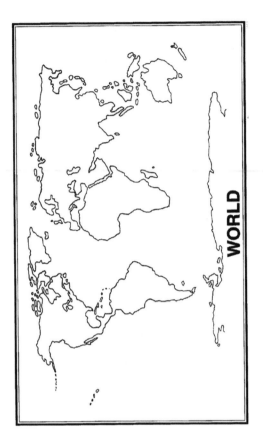

Generic Time Line

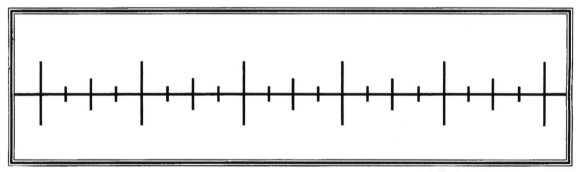

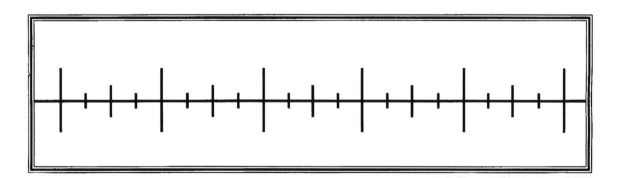

Formula Flashcards

Photocopy formula flashcards and use them for student notetaking, review, and self-testing. Flashcards can be stored in multiple pocketbooks.

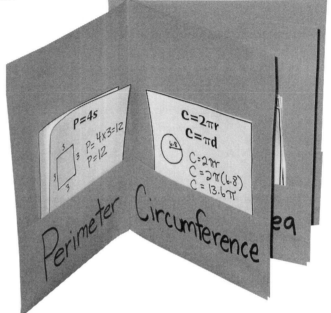

Perimeter

P=4s
square

P=2l+2w **P=2(l+w)**
rectangle

Circumference

Area

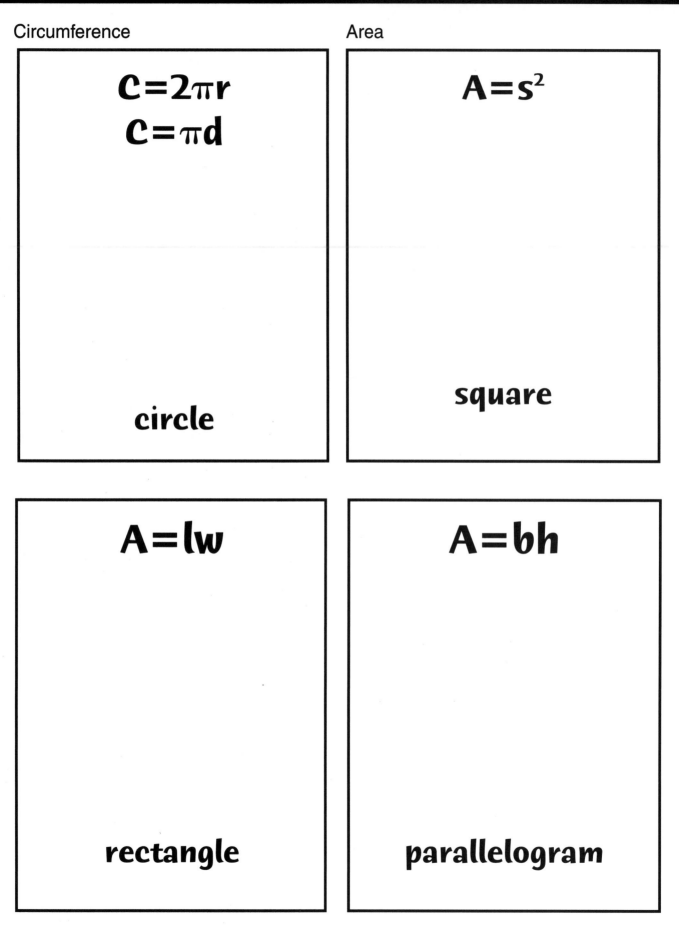

$$C=2\pi r$$
$$C=\pi d$$

circle

$$A=s^2$$

square

$$A=lw$$

rectangle

$$A=bh$$

parallelogram

$$A = \frac{1}{2}bh$$

triangle

$$A = \frac{1}{2}h(b_1 + b_2)$$

trapezoid

Surface Area

$$A = \pi r^2$$

circle

$$S = 6s^2$$

cube

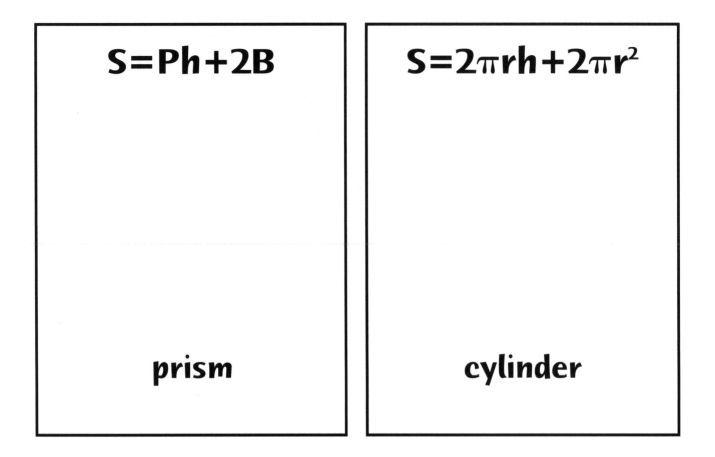

$$S = Ph + 2B$$

prism

$$S = 2\pi rh + 2\pi r^2$$

cylinder

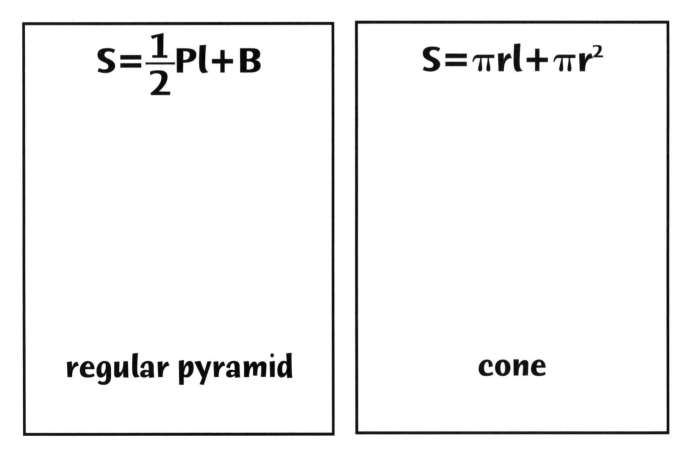

$$S = \frac{1}{2}Pl + B$$

regular pyramid

$$S = \pi rl + \pi r^2$$

cone

Lateral Area

$$S = 4\pi r^2$$

sphere

$$L = 4s^2$$

cube

$$L = ph$$

right prism

$$L = 2\pi rh$$

right circular cylinder

$$L = \frac{1}{2}Pl$$

regular pyramid

$$L = \pi rl$$

cone

Volume

$$V = s^3$$

cube

$$V = Bh$$

prism

$$V = \pi r^2 h$$

cylinder

$$V = \frac{1}{3}Bh$$

regular pyramid

$$V = \frac{1}{3}\pi r^2 h$$

cone

$$V = \frac{4}{3}\pi r^3$$

sphere

Property Sentence Strips

1. Photocopy property sentence strips on 8 1/2"x11" paper.

2. Cut along dotted lines.

3. Fold along solid lines

4. Place the sentence strips side-by-side and staple them together along the left side. See page 34 for examples of other sentence strip books.

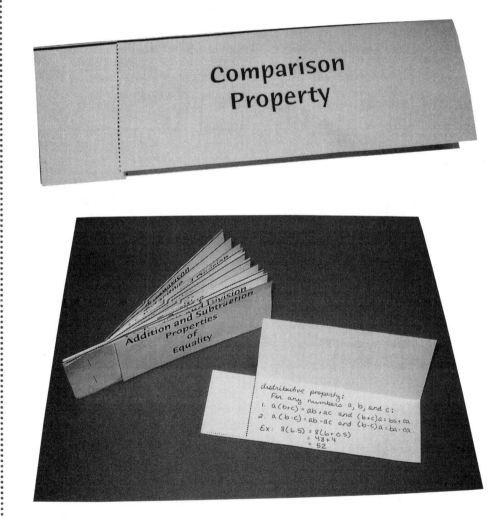

Substitution Property of Equality

Reflexive Property of Equality

Symmetric
Property
of
Equality

Transitive
Property
of
Equality

Additive
Identity
Property

Multiplicative
Identity
Property

Commutative
Property
of
Addition and Multiplication

Associative
Property
of
Addition and Multiplication

Distributive
Property

Comparison
Property

Addition and Subtraction
Properties
of
Equality

Addition and Subtraction
Properties
of
Inequality

Multiplication and Division
Properties
of
Inequality

Multiplication and Division
Properties
of
Equality

Mathematicians:
Who, What, When, Where

Use four-door books and top-tab books
to report on the lives and contributions
of important mathematicians.
*See pages 93-96 for useful graphics: maps,
time lines, and picture frames.*

Diophantus

who

when

3rd
Century

wrote:
Arithmetica

what

where

Greece

Who | what | When | Where

Blaise Pascal

WHO:

Francois
Viete

WHAT:

Symbolic
Algebra

WHEN:

(1540-1603)

WHERE:

France

January

January 1
Boris Vladimirovich Gnedenko (1912-1995), Russia

January 2
Anatoly Samoilenko, (1938-   ), Ukraine

January 3
Louis Poinsot (1777-1859), France

January 4
Sir Isaac Newton (1643-1727) England

January 5
Federigo Enriques (1871-1946), Italy

January 6
Friedrich Otto Rudolf Sturm (1841-1919),
Breslau, Germany, now Wroclaw, Poland

January 7
Gordon Thomas Whyburn (1904-1969), USA

January 8
Stephen William Hawking (1942) England

January 9
Chidambaram Padmanabhan Ramanujam (1938-1974),
India

January 10
Ruth Moufang (1905-1977), Germany

January 11
Vincenzo Riccati (1707-1775), Italy

January 12
Gregorio Ricci-Curbastro (1853-1925) Lugo, Papal
States (now Italy)

January 13
François-Félix Tisserand (1845-1896), France

January 14
Alfred Tarski (1902-1983) Warsaw, Russian Empire
(now Poland)

January 15
Sofia Vasilyevna Kovalevskaya (1850-1891), Moscow,
Russia

January 16
William Werner Boone (1920-1983), USA.

January 17
Ralph Fowler (1889-1944), England

January 18
Paul Ehrenfest (1880-1933), Austria

January 19
Guido Fubini (1879-1943) Italy

January 20
André Marie Ampère (1775-1836), France

January 21
René-Louis Baire (1874-1932), France

January 22
Leonard Eugene Dickson (1874 - 1954), USA

January 23
Michael James Lighthill (1924-1998), France

January 24
Abram Samoilovitch Besicovitch (1891-1970), Russia

January 25
Robert Boyle (1627-1691), Ireland

January 26
Eliakim Hastings Moore (1862-1932), USA

January 27
Charles Lutwidge Dodgson (1832-1898), England

January 28
Ludolph van Ceulen (1540-1610), Germany

January 29
Ernst Eduard Kummer (1810-1893), Sorau,
Brandenburg, Prussia (now Germany)

January 30
Edward Sang (1805-1890), Scotland

January 31
Lev Arkad'evich Kaluznin (1914-1990), Russia

February

February 1
John Charles Burkill (1900-1993), England

February 2
Joseph Henry Maclagen Wedderburn (1882-1948), Scotland

February 3
Pavel Samuilovich Urysohn (1898-1924), Ukraine

February 4
Chris Zeeman (1925 -) England

February 5
Wilhelm Magnus (1907-1990) Germany

February 6
Antoine Arnauld (1612-1694) in Brussels, Spanish Netherlands (now Belgium)

February 7
Godfrey Harold Hardy (1877-1947) England

February 8
Proclus Diadochus (411-485), Constantinople (now Istanbul), Byzantium (now Turkey)

February 9
Alexander Dinghas (1908-1974) Smyrna (now Izmir), Turkey

February 10
Aida Yasuaki (1747-1817) Japan

February 11
Josiah Willard Gibbs (1839-1903) USA

February 12
Hanna Neumann (1914-1971) Germany

February 13
Johann Peter Gustav Lejeune Dirichlet (1805-1859), in Düren, French Empire (now Germany)

February 14
Edward Arthur Milne (1896-1950) England

February 15
Hieronymous Georg Zeuthen (1839-1920) Denmark

February 16
Georg Joachim von Lauchen Rheticus (1514-1574) in Feldkirch, Austria

February 17
Rózsa Péter (1905-1977) in Hungary

February 18
Nasir al-Din al-Tusi (1201-1274) Tus, Khorasan (now Iran)

February 19
Axel Thue (1863-1922) Norway

February 20
Ludwig Boltzmann (1844-1906) Austria

February 21
Girard Desargues (1591-1661) France

February 22
Frank Plumpton Ramsey (1903-1930) England

February 23
Shigefumi Mori (1951) Japan

February 24
Max Black (1909-1988) Azerbaijan

February 25
Kenjiro Shoda (1902-1977) Japan

February 26
Dominique François Jean Arago (1786-1853) France

February 27
Luitzen Egbertus Jan Brouwer (1881-1966) Netherlands

February 28
Florian Cajori (1859-1930) Switzerland

February 29
Herman Hollerith (1860-1929) U.S.A.

March

March 1
Paul Dubreil (1904-1994), France

March 2
Clifford Hugh Dowker (1912-1982), Canada

March 3
Georg Ferdinand Ludwig Philipp Cantor (1845-1918) Russia

March 4
Józef Marcinkiewicz (1910-1940) Poland

March 5
Gerardus Mercator (1512-1594) Rupelmonde, Flanders (now Belgium)

March 6
Ettore Bortolotti (1866-1940) Bologna, Italy

March 7
Geoffrey Ingram Taylor (1886-1975) England

March 8
George Chrystal (1851-1911) Scotland

March 9
Howard Hathaway Aiken (1900-1973) USA

March 10
John Playfair (1748-1819) Scotland

March 11
August Leopold Crelle (1780-1855) Germany

March 12
Gustav Robert Kirchhoff (1824-1887) Prussia

March 13
Jules Joseph Drach (1871-1941) France

March 14
Albert Einstein (1879-1955) Germany

March 15
Grace Chisholm Young (1868-1944) England

March 16
Georg Simon Ohm (1789-1854) Bavaria

March 17
Wolfang Doeblin (1915-1940) Germany

March 18
Joseph Emile Barbier (1839-1889) France

March 19
Jacob Wolfowitz (1910-1981) Russian Poland

March 20
Franz Mertens (1840-1927) Prussia

March 21
Jean Baptiste Joseph Fourier (1768-1830) France

March 22
Lorna Mary Swain (1891-1936) England

March 23
Emmy Amalie Noether (1882-1935) Germany

March 24
Harold Calvin Marston Morse (1892-1977) USA

March 25
Christopher Clavius (1538-1612) Bamberg

March 26
Theodore Samuel Motzkin (1908-1970) Germany

March 27
Douglas Rayner Hartree (1897-1958) England

March 28
Israel Nathan Herstein (1923-1988) Poland

March 29
Francesco Faà di Bruno (1825-1888) Italy

March 30
Stefan Banach (1892-1945) Austria-Hungary

March 31
Etienne Bézout (1730-1783) France

April

April 1
Marie-Sophie Germain (1776-1831) France

April 2
Skokichi Iyanaga (1906-   ) Japan

April 3
Stanislaw Marcin Ulam (1909-1984) Austrian Empire

April 4
François Edouard Anatole Lucas (1842-1891) France

April 5
Honoré Fabri (1607-1688) Italy

April 6
Niels Henrik Abel (1802-1829) Norway

April 7
Erik Ivar Fredholm (1866-1927) Sweden

April 8
Marshall Harvey Stone (1903-1989) USA

April 9
Alfred Theodore Brauer (1894-1985) Germany

April 10
Henry Ernest Dudeney (1857-1930) England

April 11
Henry Scheffé (1907-1977) USA

April 12
Germinal Pierre Dandelin (1794-1847) France

April 13
Francesco Severi (1879-1961) Italy

April 14
Christiaan Huygens (1621-1695) Netherlands

April 15
Leonardo da Vinci (1452-1519) Italy

April 16
Alfred Young (1873-1940) England

April 17
Etienne Bobillier (1798-1840) France

April 18
Lars Valerian Ahlfors (1907-1996) Helsingfors, Finland, Russian Empire (now Helsinki, Finland)

April 19
Richard von Mises (1883-1953)Austria (now Lvov, Ukraine)

April 20
Francesco Siacci (1839-1907)Italy

April 21
Teiji Takagil (1875-1960) Japan

April 22
Harald August Bohr (1887-1951) Denmark

April 23
Max Karl Ernst Ludwig Planck (1858-1947) Germany

April 24
Oscar Zariski (1899-1986) Russian Empire

April 25
Andrey Nikolaevich Kolmogorov (1903-1987) Russia

April 26
Ludwig Josef Johann Wittgenstein (1889-1951) Austria

April 27
Paul Albert Gordan (1837-1912) Breslau, Germany (now Wroclaw, Poland)

April 28
Kurt Gödel (1906-1978) Brünn, Austria-Hungary (now Brno, Czech Republic)

April 29
Jules Henri Poincaré (1854-1912) France

April 30
Johann Carl Friedrich Gauss (1777-1855) Brunswick, Duchy of Brunswick (now Germany)

May

May 1
Evelyn Boyd Granville (1924-   ) USA

May 2
D'Arcy Wentworth Thompson (1860-1948) Scotland

May 3
Vito Volterra (1860-1940) Ancona, Papal States (now Italy)

May 4
William Kingdon Clifford (1845-1879) England

May 5
Cathleen Synge Morawetz (1923-   ) Canada

May 6
Willem de Sitter (1872-1934) Netherlands

May 7
Alexis Claude Clairaut (1713-1765) France

May 8
Karol Borsuk (1905-1982) Poland

May 9
Gaspard Monge (1746-1818) France

May 10
Augustin Jean Fresnel (1788-1827) France

May 11
Edna Ernestine Kramer Lassar (1902-1984) USA

May 12
Florence Nightingale (1820-1910) Italy

May 13
Lazare Nicolas Marguérite Carnot (1753-1823) France

May 14
Archie Alphonso Alexander (1888-1958) USA

May 15
Brian Hartley (1939-1994) England

May 16
Pafnuty Lvovich Chebyshev (1821-1894) Russia

May 17
Alexis Claude Clairaut (1713-1765) France

May 18
Omar Khayyam (1048-1131) in Nishapur, Persia (now Iran)

May 19
Edmond Bour (1832-1866) France

May 20
Henry Seely White (1861-11943) USA

May 21
Gaspard Gustave de Coriolis (1792-1843) France

May 22
Alfred Cardew Dixon (1865-1936) England

May 23
Lipman Bers (1914-1993) Riga, Russia (now Latvia)

May 24
Wladyslaw Orlicz (1903-1990) Okocim, Galicia, Austria-Hungary (now Poland)

May 25
Karl Mikhailovich Peterson (1828-1881) Riga, Russia (now Latvia)

May 26
Otto Neugebauer (1899-1990) Austria

May 27
Karl Johannes Herbert Seifert (19071996) Saxony

May 28
Hans Zassenhaus (1912-1991) Germany

May 29
Erwin Finlay Freundlich (1885-1964) Germany

May 30
Eugène Charles Catalan (1814-1894) Belgium

May 31
John Kemeny (1926-1992) Hungary

June

June 1
Sadi Nicolas Léonard Carnot (1796-1832) France

June 2
Tibor Radó (1895-1965) Hungary

June 3
David Gregory (1659-1708) Scotland

June 4
John Henry Pratt (1809-1871) England

June 5
John Couch Adams (1819-1892) England

June 6
Max August Zorn (1906-1993) Germany

June 7
Edward Burr Van Vleck (1863-1943) USA

June 8
Giovanni Domenico Cassini (1625-1712) Perinaldo,
Republic of Genoa (now Italy)

June 9
John Edensor Littlewood (1885-1977) England

June 10
Mohammad Abu'l-Wafa Al-Buzjani (940-998) Buzjan,
Khorasan region (now in Iran)

June 11
Charles René Reyneau (1656-1728) France

June 12
Zygmunt Janiszewski (1888-1920) Poland

June 13
John Forbes Nash (1928-   ) USA

June 14
Nilakantha Somayaji (1444-1544) Trkkantiyur (near
Tirur), Kerala, India

June 15
Nikolai Grigorievich Chebotaryov (1894-1947) Ukraine

June 16
John Wilder Tukey (1915-2000) USA

June 17
Maurits Cornelius Escher (1898-1972) Netherlands

June 18
Charles Ernest Weatherburn (1884-1974) Australia

June 19
Blaise Pascal (1623-1662) France

June 20
Helena Rasiowa (1917-1994) Austria

June 21
Siméon Denis Poisson (1781-1840) France

June 22
Hermann Minkowski (1864-1909) Alexotas, Russian
Empire (now Kaunas, Lithuania)

June 23
Alan Mathison Turing (1912-1954) England

June 24
Oswald Veblen (1880-1960) USA

June 25
Willard Van Orman Quine (1908-2000) USA

June 26
William Thomson (Lord Kelvin) 1824-1907) Ireland

June 27
Augustus De Morgan (1806-1871) in Madura, Madras
Presidency, India (now Madurai, Tamil Nadu, India)

June 28
Einar Carl Hille (1894-1980) USA

June 29
Witold Hurewicz (1904-1956) Lodz, Russian Empire
(now Poland)

June 30
Gheorghe Vranceanu (1900-1979) Romania

July

July 1
Gottfried Wilhelm von Leibniz (1646-1716) Leipzig, Saxony (now Germany)

July 2
William Burnside (1852-1927) England

July 3
Jesse Douglas (1897-1965) USA

July 4
Mikhail Samuilovich Livsic (1917-   ) Ukraine

July 5
René-Louis Baire (1874-1932) France

July 6
Alfred Bray Kempe (1849-1922) England

July 7
Johann Rudolf Wolf (1816-1893) Switzerland

July 8
Christian Kramp (1760-1826) France

July 9
George Howard Darwin (1845-1912) England

July 10
Oliver Dimon Kellogg (1878-1932) USA

July 11
Sir Joseph Larmor (1857-1942) Ireland

July 12
Richard Buckminster Fuller (1895-1983) USA

July 13
John Dee (1527-1609) England

July 14
Augustin Jean Fresnel (1788-1827) France

July 15
Stephen Smale (1930-   ) USA

July 16
Irmgard Flügge-Lotz (1903-1974) Germany

July 17
Wilhelm Lexis (1837-1914) Germany

July 18
Hendrik Antoon Lorentz (1853-1928) Netherlands

July 19
Aleksandr Yakovlevich Khinchin (1894-1959) Russia

July 20
John Playfair (1748-1819) Scotland

July 21
John Leech (1926-1992) England

July 22
Gabriel Lamé (1795-1870) France

July 23
Etienne Louis Malus (1775-1812) France

July 24
Charles Emile Picard (1856-1941) France

July 25
Johann Benedict Listing (1808-1882) Germany

July 26
Kurt Mahler (1903-1988) Prussian Rhineland

July 27
Johann Bernoulli (1667-1748) Switzerland

July 28
Gerd Faltings (1954-   ) Germany

July 29
Sir Ronald Aylmer Fisher (1890-1962) England

July 30
Julia Hall Bowman Robinson (1919-1985) USA

July 31
Gabriel Cramer (1704-1752) Switzerland

August

August 1
Ivar Otto Bendixson (1861-1935) Sweden

August 2
Oskar Johann Viktor Anderson (1887-1960) Belarus

August 3
George Francis FitzGerald (1851-1901) Ireland

August 4
John Venn (1834-1923) England

August 5
Niels Henrik Abel (1802 1829) Norway

August 6
Nicolas Malebranche (1638-1715), France

August 7
Ladislaus Josephowitsch Bortkiewicz (1868-1931)
Russia

August 8
Paul Adrien Maurice Dirac (1902-1984) England

August 9
Franciscus Barocius (1537-1604) Crete

August 10
Carol Ruth Karp (1926-1972) USA

August 11
Norman Levinson (1912-1975) USA

August 12
Erwin Rudolf Josef Alexander Schrödinger (1887-1961)
Austria

August 13
George Gabriel Stokes (1819-1903) Ireland

August 14
Charles Jean Gustave Nicolas Baron de la Vallée
Poussin
(1866-1962) Belgium

August 15
Louis Victor Pierre Raymond duc de Broglie (1892-
1987) France

August 16
Arthur Cayley (1821-1895) England

August 17
Pierre de Fermat (1601-1665) France

August 18
Brook Taylor (1685-1731) England

August 19
Alan Baker (1939-   ) England

August 20
Simon Kirwan Donaldson (1957-   ) England

August 21
Augustin Louis Cauchy (1789-1857) France

August 22
Denis Papin (1647-1712) France

August 23
John Arthur Todd (1908-1994) England

August 24
Karen Keskulla Uhlenbeck (1942-   ) USA

August 25
Helmut Hasse (1898-1979) Germany

August 26
Wolfgang Krull (1899-1971) Germany

August 27
Giuseppe Peano (1858-1932) Italy

August 28
Shizuo Kakutani (1911   ) Japan

August 29
Leonard Roth (1904-1968) England

August 30
Olga Taussky-Todd (1906-   ) Olmütz, Austro-Hungarian
Empire (now Olomouc, Czech Republic)

August 31
Hermann Ludwig Ferdinand von Helmholtz (1821-1894)
Germany

September

September 1
Pao-Lu Hsu (1910-1970) China

September 2
Israil Moiseevic Gelfand (1913....) Ukraine

September 3
Lev Semenovich Pontryagin (1908-1988) Russia

September 4
Luigi Federico Menabrea (1809-1896) France

September 5
Jean Etienne Montucla (1725-1799) France

September 6
Maurice George Kendall (1907-1983) England

September 7
Georges Louis Leclerc Comte de Buffon (1707-1788) France

September 8
Marin Mersenne (1588-1648) France

September 9
Marjorie Lee Browne (1914-1979) USA

September 10
Georges de Rham (1903-1990) Switzerland

September 11
Kenkichi Iwasawa (1917-1998) Japan

September 12
Antoine-André-Louis Reynaud (1771-1844) France

September 13
Constantin Carathéodory (1873-1950) Germany

September 14
Alberto P Calderón (1920-1998) Argentina

September 15
Abu Arrayhan Muhammad ibn Ahmad al-Biruni (973-1048) Kath, Khwarazm (now Kara-Kalpakskaya, Uzbekistan)

September 16
Francisco Maurolico (1494-1575) Italy

September 17
Georg Friedrich Bernhard Riemann (1826-1866) Breselenz, Hanover (now Germany)

September 18
Adrien-Marie Legendre (1752-1833) France

September 19
James Waddell Alexander (1888-1971) USA

September 20
Erich Hecke (1887-1947) Buk, Posen, Germany (now Poznan, Poland)

September 21
Juliusz Pawel Schauder (1899-1943) Lvov, Galicia, Austria-Hungary (now Ukraine)

September 22
Paolo Ruffini (1765-1822) Valentano, Papal States (now Italy)

September 23
David van Dantzig (1900-1959) Netherlands

September 24
Girolamo Cardano (1501-1576) Pavia, Duchy of Milan (now Italy)

September 25
Alexander Markowich Ostrowski (1893-1986) Ukraine

September 26
Percy Alexander MacMahon (1854-1929) Malta

September 27
Paul Emile Appell (1855-1930) France

September 28
Julian Lowell Coolidge (1873-1954) USA

September 29
Adriaan van Roomen (1561-1615) Belgium

September 30
Samuel Eilenberg (1913-1998) Poland

October

October 1
Luigi Guido Grandi (1671-1742) Italy

October 2
Arthur Erdélyi (1908-1977) Hungary

October 3
194Pierre René Deligne (1944-   ) Belgium

October 4
Louis François Antoine Arbogast (1759-1803) Alsace

October 5
Bernard Placidus Johann Nepomuk Bolzano (1781-1848) Prague, Bohemia, Austrian Habsburg domain (now Czech Republic)

October 6
Julius Wihelm Richard Dedekind (1831-1916) Braunschweig, duchy of Braunschweig (now Germany)

October 7
Niels Henrik David Bohr (1885-1962) Denmark

October 8
Hans Arnold Heilbronn (1908-1975) Germany

October 9
Benjamin Banneker (1731-1806) USA

October 10
Heinrich Friedrich Karl Ludwig Burkhardt (1861-1914) Germany

October 11
Cahit Arf (1910-1997) Salonika, Ottoman Empire (now Thessaloniki, Greece)

October 12
Piero della Francesca (1412-1492) Italy

October 13
John Griggs Thompson (1932-   ) USA

October 14
Robert Simson (1687-1768) Scotland

October 15
Evangelista Torricelli (1608-1647) Faenza, Romagna (now Italy)

October 16
Philip Edward Bertrand Jourdain (1879-1921) England

October 17
Paul Isaac Bernays (1888-1977) England

October 18
Margaret Dusa Waddington McDuff (1945-   ) England

October 19
Jean Frédéric Auguste Delsarte (Oct 1903-1968) France

October 20
Sir Christopher Wren (1632-1723) England

October 21
Enrico Betti (1823-1892) Pistoia, Tuscany (now Italy)

October 22
Joachim Jungius (1587-1657) Germany

October 23
Piers Bohl (1865-1921) Walka, Livonia (now Valka, Latvia)

October 24
Aleksandr Osipovich Gelfond (1906-1968) Russia

October 25
Evariste Galois (1811-1832) France

October 26
Ferdinand Georg Frobenius (1849-1917) Berlin-Charlottenburg, Prussia (now Germany)

October 27
Robert Alexander Rankin (1915-2001) Scotland

October 28
Pierre François Verhulst (1804-1849) Belgium

October 29
Klaus Friedrich Roth (1925-   ) Breslau, Germany (now Wroclaw, Poland)

October 30
Andrei Nikolaevich Tikhonov (1906-1993) Russia

October 31
Karl Theodor Wilhelm Weierstrass (1815-1897) Ostenfelde, Westphalia (now Germany)

November

November 1
Giambattista Della Porta (1535-1615) Italy

November 2
George Boole (1815-1864) England

November 3
Arthur Byron Coble (1878-1966) USA

November 4
Pierre Simon Girard (1765-1836) France

November 5
Robert Wayne Thomason (1952-1995) USA

November 6
Giovanni Antonio Amedeo Plana (1781-1864) Italy

November 7
Raphaël Salem (1898-1963) Greece

November 8
Edmond Halley (1656-1742) England

November 9
Abraham Adrian Albert (1905-1972) USA

November 10
Elwin Bruno Christoffel (1829-1900) Germany

November 11
Louis Antoine de Bougainville (1729-1811) France

November 12
John William Strutt Lord Rayleigh (1842-1919) England

November 13
Ernest Julius Wilczynski (1876-1932) Germany

November 14
Ulisse Dini (1845-1918) Italy

November 15
David George Crighton (1942-2000) Wales

November 16
Eugenio Beltrami (1835-1900) Cremona, Lombardy, Austrian Empire (now Italy)

November 17
Jean Le Rond d'Alembert (1717-1783) France

November 18
Shigeo Sasaki (1912-   ) Japan

November 19
Heinz Hopf (1894-1971) Gräbschen, Germany (now Wroclaw, Poland)

November 20
Edwin Powell Hubble (1889-1953) USA

November 21
Dmitrii Sintsov (1867-1946) Russia

November 22
F Burton Jones (1910-1999) USA

November 23
John Wallis (1616-1703) England

November 24
Gerhard Gentzen (1909-1945) Germany

November 25
Friedrich Wilhelm Karl Ernst Schröder (1841-1902) Germany

November 26
Norbert Wiener (1894-1964) USA

November 27
Anatoly Ivanovich Malcev (1909-1967) Russia

November 28
John Wishart (1898-1956) Scotland

November 29
Christian Andreas Doppler (1803-1853) Austria

November 30
Sir Henry Savile (1549-1622) England

December

December 1
Nikolai Ivanovich Lobachevsky (1792-1856) Russia

December 2
Paul David Gustav Du Bois-Reymond (1831-1889) Germany

December 3
John Backus (1924-   ) USA

December 4
Ludwig Georg Elias Moses Bieberbach (1886-1982) Germany

December 5
Werner Karl Heisenberg (1901-1976) Germany

December 6
Giulio Carlo Fagnano dei Toschi (1682-1766) Italy

December 7
Leopold Kronecker (1823-1891) Liegnitz, Prussia (now Legnica, Poland)

December 8
Jacques Salomon Hadamard (1865-1963) France

December 9
Grace Brewster Murray Hopper (1906-1992) USA

December 10
Augusta Ada King, countess of Lovelace (1815-1852) England

December 11
Max Born (1882-1970) Breslau, Germany (now Wroclaw, Poland)

December 12
Peter Ludwig Mejdell Sylow (1832-1918) Norway

December 13
George Pólya (1887-1985) Hungary

December 14
Tycho Brahe (1546-1601) Denmark

December 15
János Bolyai (1802-1860) Kolozsvár, Austrian Empire (now Cluj, Romania)

December 16
Viktor Yakovlevich Bunyakovsky (1804-1889) Ukraine

December 17
Marius Sophus Lie (1842-1899) Norway

December 18
Roger C Lyndon (1917-1988) USA

December 19
Helmut Wielandt (1910-2001) Germany

December 20
Paul Tannery (1843-1904) France

December 21
Jan Lukasiewicz (1878-1956) Lvov, Austrian Galicia (now Ukraine)

December 22
Srinivasa Aiyangar Ramanujan (1887-1920) India

December 23
Georgii Yurii Pfeiffer (1872-1946) Ukraine

December 24
Charles Hermite (1822-1901) France

December 25
Antoni Zygmund (1900-1992) Warsaw, Russian Empire (now Poland)

December 26
Mary Fairfax Greig Somerville (1780-1872) Scotland

December 27
Johannes Kepler (1571-1630) Weil der Stadt, Württemberg, Holy Roman Empire (now Germany)

December 28
John von Neumann (1903-1957) Hungary

December 29
Thomas Jan Stieltjes (1856-1894) The Netherlands

December 30
Stanislaw Saks (1897-1942) Poland

December 31
Carl Ludwig Siegel (1896-1981) Germany

Index

Workshops and Keynote Presentations

Dinah's presentations give participants an unprecedented opportunity to meet and work with the designer as she shares her internationally renowned, three-dimensional, interactive graphic organizers. Teachers learn how to make class work, projects, assessment, and note taking unforgettable visual and kinesthetic experiences. Dinah's Foldables™ can be used by students and teachers in all grade levels and subjects.

Workshops

For more information on Dinah Zike's workshops and keynote presentations, contact Cecile Stepman at **1-210-698-0123** or **cecile@dinah.com**.

Orders

To receive a free catalog or to order other books by Dinah Zike, call **1-800-99DINAH** or email at **orders@dinah.com**.

E-Group

To join Dinah Zike's e-group and receive new activity ideas, send an email to **mindy@dinah.com** or sign up on our website at **www.dinah.com**.

Watch for new and upcoming books in Dinah Zike's Big Book series!

Each book in Dinah's Big Book series is subject specific and features instructions for approximately thirty graphic organizers, 100 full-color photographed examples, five black-line art examples per page, and thousands of graphic organizer ideas for teaching.

Please check our website at www.dinah.com or call 210-698-0123 for availability of books for the following subjects:

Elementary
Dinah Zike's Big Book of...
Social Studies
Texas History (K-7)
Math
Science
Health
Art History
English

Middle School and High School
Dinah Zike's Big Book of...
Science
Math
American History
World History
Geography
English